Thanks taking to listen / :)

Dr. John

"I WANT TO HEAR YOU"

22 TIPS FOR ARTFUL LISTENING BEFORE, DURING, AND AFTER A CONVERSATION

John G. Igwebuike, Ph.D., J.D.

with

Peter R. Malik, Ph.D.

"I Want to Hear You": 22 Tips for Artful Listening before, during, and after a Conversation

Written by John G. Igwebuike, Ph.D., J.D. with Peter R. Malik, Ph.D

First edition. November, 2020

Website: www.leadlisteninginstitute.com

Contact: Please contact the author through the organization's website located at www.leadlisteninginstitute.com.

ISBN: 978-0-9710037-3-6

Listening is at the root of
everything: all learning,
relationships, spirituality, laughter,
length of life, and love.
One of the greatest things we can do
is to show speakers that we are
artfully listening; this demonstrates
to them that they too are capable of
listening artfully.

Guanacaste
THE LEAD LISTENING INSTITUTE

CONTENTS

Part III: AFTER THE CONVERSATION 81

Acknowledgements

I have been on the listening journey for nearly 25 years, and I thank God for seeding within me the mission to teach people how to improve their lives through the positive power of listening. To the Guanacastes in my life—some of you are newly sown seeds in the rich fertile soil of earthy listening knowledge; others are seedlings just bursting from the soil; and others of you are sprouts, saplings, small trees, or seed-bearing Guanacaste trees.

Wherever you are in your listening growth trajectory, I want to thank you—Guanacastes—for your support during my quest to enhance receptive excellence. You have given shade, sunshine, nutrients, rain, fertilizer, and a gentle breeze. You have provided prayers, referrals, speaking engagements, training opportunities, encouragement, and support.

I give very special thanks to my wonderful wife, Sharon, "the superwoman." My wife has often referred to herself as my LGP (Listening Guinea Pig) because very often I have shared with her numerous ideas, seminar topics, and illustrations for her thoughts, ideas, and feedback. Also, my dazzling, darling daughters Neziah, Naomi, and Natalia have provided the inspiration and support to produce this work. Neziah, my oldest daughter and a budding writer in her own right, read the entire manuscript of this book and offered her insightful critique.

I would also like to thank my dear friend, Dr. Peter R. Malik, who has been invaluable in helping me finish this book, an important part of the listening work. This book would not have been possible without his wise counsel, exuberant collaboration, and indefatigable commitment. Thank you, Peter! I would also like to express my appreciation to Dr. Chris Gilmer, Dr. Sarah C. Johnson and Gregg McMurtrie who reviewed an early draft of this book.

In addition, certain individuals have been "supererogatory" = going above and beyond the call of duty to support and advance this "listening work": Dr. Eddie Moore, Jr. of the Privilege Institute, Madame Nicci Wangerin, Dr. Michelle Lee, Dr. Donna Williams, Supreme Lady Micaela LeBlanc, Derius Swinton, Al Duncan, Pamela A. Bivens, Tamara Gibson, Ralph Smithers, Dr. Alvin T. Simpson, Dr. James Moore III, Dr. C. Edward Rhodes II, John White, Kyle Marshall, Bertie Ford, Dr. Rebecca Fairchild, Dr. Debra Spring, Dr. Tracee Smith, Edith Riley, Bishop Curtis Smith and Prophetess LaToyia Smith, Julia Odom, Tamara Foster-Montgomery, Dr. W. Franklin Evans, Truvaunda Bass, Dr. Samuel Jones, Dr. Thomas Sturgis, Dr. Jason Cable, Dr. and Mrs. Girish Panicker, Dr. Benedict Udemgba, Pebbles Epps, Joseph Dimpah, Dr. Valerie Thompson, Dr. Kendall Isaac, Dr. Steve Adzanu, Dr. Jermiah Billa, Michael Atkins, and so many more.

Without a doubt, my beloved parents, (Godwin and Kate Igwebuike and R. G. and Costella Terrell), brothers (Eboh, Alvin, Leo, Rick, and Craig) and sisters (Ada, Uche, Valerie, and Hannah) as well as extended family have been, are, and continue to be eternal inspirations. Finally, my listening audiences have helped me grow "tree"-mendously. You have all been great Guanacastes, "Listening Trees," and I love each of you. I want to hear you!

A Message from the Author

On a trip I took to Costa Rica some years ago, I saw the beautiful beaches, lovely landscapes, and verdant vistas. Most significantly, I had the life-changing opportunity to see the abundant acreage dotted with tall, tremendous trees called the Guanacastes. Guanacaste means Listening Tree. It is the native tree of Costa Rica ("rich coast") and the country's national tree. The Guanacaste has a broad canopy of green leaves and produces bright, brown seed pods that look like the human ear.

My travel to Costa Rica coalesced with a growth journey I have been on for nearly 25 years: a lifelong commitment to help people improve their ability to connect verbally and nonverbally with others on a deep and profound level through the positive power of active listening. In fact, the image of the Guanacaste and its pods containing seeds which are frequently worn as jewelry has been adapted as the logo for The Lead Listening Institute which I founded. It portrays the image that, under the Guanacaste tree, we learn the craft of listening from our ancestors and adorn ourselves with the tree's mighty seeds to remind us and our descendants of the importance of listening artfully.

In my years of doing this work, I have often said that listening is the greatest skill never taught. Very few people are ever coached or counseled, educated or edified, schooled or skilled, taught or trained in the finest of the fine arts—the art of listening. The need for listening education is very real. One could get a high school diploma and not receive any schooling on why it is important to stop, look, and listen.

A person could graduate from a college or university without any formal education regarding what it means to listen to another human being with compassion, empathy, and understanding. One could acquire a graduate or professional degree and not grasp the degree to which every human being thirsts, craves, and desires to be heard. Yet, this seed is rarely planted, and, as a consequence, the landscape of human communication and connection is almost bare, barren, and bereft of Listening Trees.

With artful listening, a conversation grows into something much more—a creation made, a spark illuminated, an experience fashioned. Artful listening is a grassy spot under a shady tree; not listening is a soundproof booth. Artful listening brings connection, laughter, love, peace, respect, and understanding. Not listening (or not being listened to) can cause distance and isolation—even death. If you have ever been in a situation where you were not being heard (the listener interrupts you, looks at his or her watch, or cuts the conversation short), you know what it feels like when your "listener" lacks listening skill. Indeed, the world needs more Guanacaste trees—more artful listeners.

I want you to get so much more out of your conversations, and I hope that this book will help you do so. Why listening? Why art? Why artful listening? Listening and art are connected. They are one and the same. The word "art" is embedded within the word "heart." To separate "art" from "heart" is to leave the word "heart" incomplete. The art of listening should be at the heart of every conversation. The artful listener understands that listening occurs not just from lips to ear but heart to heart. The most important thing we can do when we listen to any person, performance, or piece of music is to have the "heart" to listen.

Beyond the ideas and insights, skills and strategies, and techniques and tips contained in this book, one's single-minded determination to focus his or her energies, thoughts, ideas, mind, and attention on the speaker is the sine qua non of artful listening. Yet, I can already hear what you're saying right now: "Wait a minute," you say. "That's insane. What planet are you from? I already know how to listen. I listen all the time—to my friends, teachers, parents, music, television, nature, everything." And I have no doubt in my mind that the words and sounds that you do hear every day actually reach your ears. However, I invite you to answer three questions:

Are you doing more than just hearing?

Are you optimizing your conversations with people?

Are you getting the most out of your listening experiences?

I humbly suggest that you most likely are not making the most of your listening moments with others. I sincerely want to help you become a new version of yourself by instilling in you a deep, abiding understanding of the importance of listening, so that you can make full use of your receptive faculties. I am positive that it will do wonders for your relationships with family, friends, and coworkers.

I take the work of listening education and training very seriously. I really do. In certain cases, listening to others (and being listened to) is a matter of life and death. Hence, listening is my lifeblood, my raison d'être. I have written this book with hope that you will take listening more seriously after you have read it. For I believe to my core that listening artfully is a miracle which can be life changing, life giving, and life saving.

Now let's sit together beneath the quiet shade of the Guanacaste tree and go on a magical journey in artfully listening.

Part I:

BEFORE THE CONVERSATION

1

Tip 1:
Contact the Speaker

In some respects, getting on someone's calendar is one of the most important things that must happen prior to a conversation. In order to have a conversation with the chief executive officer of your company, for example, you must first arrange and confirm the date, time of day, location, and expected duration of the meeting with the CEO's office. Agreeing on the duration of the conversation is significant because it focuses the speaker's and listener's attention on accomplishing the goals of the conversation in the time allotted to it.

Artful listeners will go the extra mile on the day before the conversation by emailing, texting, or making a voice call to the speaker. In the communication, the artful listener will remind the speaker of the date, time, location, and duration of the conversation and ask the speaker if there is anything else that the speaker might require for the conversation. This singular step of early outreach sends a strong yet subtle signal to the speaker that the listener values the speaker's time and welcomes the opportunity for new items to be added to the agenda. Early outreach enhances the possibility of a meaningful conversation and fosters a lasting sense of goodwill that will carry over into the meeting itself.

From these two communications (reaching out to set the agenda and communicating again the day before), the listener may make notes about the speaker's responses which will be helpful to the listener before the conversation (the particularities), during the conversation (the priorities), and after the conversation (the possibilities).

Tip 2:
Remove Personal Agendas

"The purest form of listening is to listen without memory or desire."

–Wilfred Bion

Clearing your mind is the initial act of preparation for a conversation. It is helpful to decode and deconstruct the verb "prepare" with regard to your commitment to the practice of artful listening. According to Dictionary.com, the preposition "pre-" means "before" or "beforehand." The English word "pare" means "to reduce or remove by or as by cutting; diminish or decrease gradually." When the listener commits to the process of paring before a conversation, he or she is actively readying himself or herself to listen artfully to the speaker.

Much like a surgeon who prepares for an operation by disinfecting and cleaning the surgical tools, an athlete who stretches and warms up to prepare the muscles for exercise, or an artist who washes brushes and containers to prepare for painting a picture, the artful listener pre-"pares" by clearing the mind before the conversation begins of unwanted thoughts, negative emotions, irrelevant thinking, personal agendas, expectations, stereotypes, judgments, and assumptions. Eliminating these distractions increases the concentration and single-minded focus that artful listening requires.

As a prerequisite for the process of paring, an artful listener should commit himself or herself to the time-honored practice of journaling. The word "journal" comes from the Old French word "journal" meaning "daily." By keeping a journal, your commitment to artful listening is formed one day at a time. The habit of journaling is a commitment to your ongoing growth and development as an evolving expert in artful listening. Through journaling, you can easily capture whatever is on your mind. It is easy. Just free write across the page. Build the habit of journaling for 30 minutes daily. You may also do additional journaling before you have an important artful conversation such as a workplace meeting or a job interview.

Journaling will liberate your thoughts. The process can unveil and release thoughts you didn't know were there. When you journal, do not concern yourself with matters of grammar, style, penmanship, or even content. The goal is to make the invisible visible, the unexpressed expressed, and the unseen seen. Use journaling as a way to get the thoughts from your head and heart to your hand and from your hand to the page of your journal. The commitment to daily journaling will help you channel your thoughts as well as reflect and release them onto the page.

Although we live in the technology age replete with software and apps for journaling, handwriting the journal is optimal. Paper is faster, easier, and more flexible than a computer screen. With paper, you won't have any notifications popping onto your screen and distracting you.

Remember that the mind can only really think of one thing at a time. The concept of multitasking is a myth. Journaling prunes, purges, and pares the mind for focus on one thing—one thought—at a time. Writing things down in your own words can be really powerful. Journaling washes away the negative thoughts, so your true self can come forth and be heard, so that you can l-i-s-t-e-n. You may also combine journaling with other centering activities that you might do already such as exercise, stretches, and meditation.

After a month or two of daily journaling, you can then look back on your thoughts from days past and reflect on how your thinking on a particular subject has possibly changed. In this way, journaling not only helps you to collect and cultivate your thoughts but also to curate and memorialize them. In addition, journaling will help you improve your note-taking skills which, as we will see later in this book, will be of immeasurable value to you in the workplace.

M. Scott Peck noted: "We cannot let another person into our hearts or minds unless we empty ourselves." Journaling is above all an emptying process. When you journal, you are actually listening to your foremost and topmost thoughts and catching (emptying) them on paper. This will help you know yourself at a deep level. Here is a five-step system for creating and maintaining an artful listening journal:

1. Purchase a journal. This can be a spiral-bound notebook, a smaller diary-type journal with no lines, or an appointment-style calendar with lines and a separate space for each day of the year.

2. Keep your notations simple but write for 30 minutes each day.

3. Store your journal in the same place every day. This may be a drawer in a bedside table or bedroom desk; you may also choose a more secure location in your home.

4. Pick a specific time in your day when you will journal. You may journal after you awaken, before the evening meal, or just prior to bedtime.

5. Keep it up. The first few days are the most challenging.

To summarize, clearing your mind is the initial act of preparation for a conversation. To aid in the process of paring, an artful listener should commit himself or herself to daily journaling. Journaling purges and pares the mind to focus on one thing—one thought—at a time. Keeping a handwritten journal not only empowers you to empty yourself but also to hear yourself, listen to yourself, understand yourself, and know yourself. It is very helpful to follow a five-step system for creating and maintaining a daily journal.

Tip 3:
Discard Prejudgments

Carl R. Rogers and F. J. Roethlisberger wrote a seminal article in the *Harvard Business Review* (originally published in 1952 and republished in 1991) entitled "Barriers and Gateways to Communication." In their groundbreaking article, Rogers and Roethlisberger describe good communication as "free communication" and note that free communication is in itself a form of therapy. Stated differently, they consider a free flow of communication within and between people as good communication. However, Rogers and Roethlisberger go on to identify the chief barrier to this type of free communication—the tendency of people to judge others. Rogers and Roethlisberger point out that judging others stifles the exchange of ideas between persons as well as the freedom to speak freely and thereby creates a major impediment to authentic communication. Now let's discuss the two main roadblocks to free and effective communication.

Roadblock No. 1: The Listener's Prejudgments

The tendency of people to evaluate or judge others can be illustrated by the following verbal exchange between Maria and her co-worker Nora:

> Maria: "I think the government's handling of the coronavirus pandemic was insufficient."
>
> Nora (without hesitation): "Well, I thought the government did a creditable job by instituting shelter-in-place orders."

Reading this brief conversation, the artful listener first notices that Nora's comment is an evaluation. Rather than listening fully to what Maria is saying, Nora is already formulating a response to what she is hearing. A speedy, evaluative judgment like this is often ingrained in our day-to-day communication exchanges. However, the artful listener perceives the statement for what it is: an impediment to free communication—a judgment.

This rush to judgment can further be seen and illustrated in what is known as the 12 × 12 × 12 × 12 rule. The rule shows the natural human tendency to judge others. According to this rule, a person meeting a stranger makes a series of judgments regarding the stranger on a subconscious, automatic level. The stranger is first judged from 12 yards away (car), then judged from 12 feet away (clothing), and then from 12 inches away (skin color). Finally, the stranger is judged by the first 12 words (conversation) that he or she speaks. Based on this rule, the stranger only has about three seconds to make a good first impression.

Each part of the 12 × 12 × 12 × 12 rule involves a snap judgment about the stranger. The spontaneous, automatic nature of each judgment is a type of prejudgment commonly referred to as unconscious bias. This bias forms a barrier to free communication because the observer's perception is hopelessly compromised by these judgments when the conversation is barely underway.

The key to minimizing the urge to judge is to accept that we are all prone to it due to our upbringing. We hear and learn without giving the process a second thought. For example, as children, we learned our ABCs and 123s by hearing the numbering system and the alphabet repeated over and over again until those sequences became automatic in our consciousness. In a similar fashion, we learned to walk by doing it over and over again until walking became automatic. The same is true about how we learned to brush our teeth, tie our shoes, dress, and comb our hair; these routines are so automatic now that we do not give them a conscious thought. Because of the power and potential of our hearing ability to form, conform, and transform our way of thinking, our biases about people can become so deeply entrenched in our minds as children that we as adults do not examine their origin.

Advertisers tap the power of rote recall by bombarding our minds and ears with repeated slogans. You are already familiar with three of them: Nike ("Just Do It"), Visa ("It's Everywhere You Want to Be"), and Burger King ("Have It Your Way"). We recall these slogans with little effort because we've heard them consciously and subconsciously hundreds if not thousands of times. They have become second nature to us. In many instances, slogans become the basis upon which we judge products, even though the slogans actually have little to do with the value or quality of the products themselves.

Almost as fast as we recall commercial slogans, we spontaneously bring to mind the statements, evaluations, and prejudgments we have heard from childhood regarding other people. Just as slogans trigger prejudgments about products, stereotypes are created in our young minds about the value of people based on many factors such as race, gender, age, style of dress, speech pattern, diet, religion, and lifestyle. Sadly, many of these prejudgments have never been rationally analyzed by the adults who still hold them.

How does one resist the urge to judge and thereby reduce the inner tendency to evaluate others? As Rogers and Roethlisberger recommended, "If people can learn to listen with understanding, they can mitigate their evaluative impulses and greatly improve their communication with others." To lessen the tendency to evaluate, one must cultivate artful listening as opposed to simple hearing. The distinction between hearing and listening must remain at the top of one's mind.

While hearing is an automatic process that harnesses the ears' sound processing apparatus, listening is a conscious act that involves not only the ears (hearing) but also one's entire being (mind, heart, soul, and body). Hearing is natural and unlearned; listening is super-natural and must be learned and developed through practice. With the proper motivation and continual practice, a person can learn to shed stereotypes and thereby attain a more judgment-free approach to listening.

Roadblock No. 2: The Listener's Point of View

Another major roadblock in the exchange between Maria and Nora is the frame of reference from which Nora's reply emanates. When Maria hears Nora's response ("Well, I thought the government did a creditable job by instituting shelter-in-place orders"), Maria recognizes that Nora is making the statement from Nora's point of view, not Maria's. Thus, not only is Nora's counterstatement a judgment of what Maria presented, but also it is an evaluation of Maria's point of view and Maria as a person.

Nora's quick retort also represents a negative assessment that Rogers and Roethlisberger regard as another major barrier to effective communication. Nora is hearing Maria's statement solely from her (Nora's) personal point of view. Thus, the inclination to hear a speaker's statement from the listener's viewpoint rather than the *speaker's* vantage point is the second major roadblock to effective, free-flowing communication.

To counter this tendency to evaluate the speaker's comment from the listener's point of view, the artful listener applies more of the brake pedal approach than the gas pedal strategy to a conversation. Artful listening requires patience, patience, patience as well as a shift in perspective, perspective, perspective.

An artful listener chooses to travel on the communication free-way using a manual (listening) transmission rather than an automatic (hearing) transmission. Listening, like manual shifting, requires more energy and focus but ultimately results in better understanding and energy saved. Rather than reacting automatically to whatever stereotypes and hot-button words that the speaker may be espousing, the artful listener consciously downshifts to understand the speaker without precondition, prejudice, or prejudgment from the *speaker's* point of view. Such conscious perspective-taking is called empathy; to listen empathically ("with the ears of another") fosters what Rogers and Roethlisberger call good communication.

The listener garners so much understanding through careful listening that an artful shift in perspective often takes place in such a way that the listener sees things from the vantage point of the speaker. The empathetic outcome of such a speaker-focused perspective results not only in effective communication but also in conversation that is free flowing and therapeutic.

A wonderful example of listening without judging and with a speaker-focused perspective is the amazing experience of Daryl Davis, an African-American musical artist who through the years has met and befriended several members of the Ku Klux Klan. Over long conversations with the Klan members, Davis listened patiently to their statements of hate. Gradually and without malice, Davis discussed racial relations with these KKK members for many months and actually changed some of their minds about race. In fact, several of the Klan members befriended by Davis wound up leaving the Klan because they no longer adhered to its tenets.

In a research article entitled "Speaker–Listener Neural Coupling Underlies Successful Communication," Greg J. Stephens, Lauren J. Silbert and Uri Hasson stated that "verbal communication is a joint activity; however, speech production and comprehension have primarily been analyzed as independent processes within the boundaries of individual brains." The researchers then described how they recorded brain activity from both speakers and listeners during natural verbal communication: "We used the speaker's spatiotemporal brain activity to model listeners' brain activity and found that the speaker's activity is spatially and temporally coupled with the listener's activity." They also noted that "this coupling vanishes when participants fail to communicate."

These results are exciting. By examining the brain scans of a speaker who is telling a personal story to a listener who is listening well, the researchers found that the greater overlap and similarity of neural impulses between speaker and listener, the better the communication. In other words, evidence of human connection during a genuine conversation is observable and measurable. Hence, the wonderful feeling that you have when you "click" with another person during a conversation is not only emotionally palpable but also scientifically demonstrable.

The possibility of this type of deep connection has positive implications for a number of everyday relationships such as spouse-spouse, friend-friend, stranger-stranger, teacher-student, salesperson-customer, and supervisor-employee. If we set aside our preconceived notions and listen to the speaker's story from the speaker's point of view, the brain waves of the speaker and the listener will begin to couple, connect, cocreate, and click.

Artful listeners will recognize that just like there is a "sinking" feeling when they are not heard, there is a buoyant "syncing" feeling when they are heard deeply. People are social beings with a craving to connect (to be heard, listened to, and understood). One of the most complex, nuanced, and intricate things that humans are capable of doing is connecting with one another through authentic conversations. Furthermore, I believe that all people are divinely designed to do this. Here are my top tips and takeaways for discarding prejudgments:

Always Be Curious

The wisdom from the book *How to Win Friends & Influence People* by Dale Carnegie is helpful here: "Be interested, not interesting." Curate a curiosity that empowers you to take a genuine interest in the speaker and what he or she has to say. Be like a visitor to a museum examining a picture. Be interested in the shadings, texture, and colors of a painting. Just as you accept the artist's rendering in the museum (you certainly would not pull out your own paint brushes with colors to alter the artist's work), be accepting of the speaker for whom he or she is and what he or she wants to share with you. Think ABC (Always Be Curious) when you listen.

Seek the Speaker's Stories

One way to mitigate the impulse to evaluate or prejudge a speaker is to seek the speaker's stories. To connect deeply with another's story, you must offer your undivided attention and an open mind. What you learn can surprise you and counter stereotypes, explode myths, and expose you to altogether different ways of seeing the world and other people. Asking a coworker how he or she is doing—and then attentively listening—can be a window to eliciting an important story from him or her. Everybody has a story to tell, and he or she is thirsting to share it with people who listen artfully, openly, and nonjudgmentally.

Avoid Judgment

Remember that your goal is to listen artfully to what the speaker is seeking to say. This means that you must understand the speaker's perspective and accept it for what it is, even if it clashes with your own worldview. Remember that to interrupt or quickly respond with counter arguments, counter points, and counter perspectives is not listening with art or grace. To listen artfully (heartfully), aim to take on the speaker's mindset as a child would. Suspend all judgment and react to each new bit of information as if it were a revelation and a blessing. Become a humble student of the speaker, not a judge or jury.

Listen like a Child

Consider the child who comes home from school and says, "I met a new friend today." The friend may be of a different race, religion, ethnicity, or socioeconomic class, but the child is not attuned to that. Ironically, children are often the ones most capable of giving the gift of their authentic, nonjudgmental selves to people who are of different ages, races, and life experiences. Sadly, many adults have lost this capability. Let us listen with childlike acceptance.

Stand Under = Understand

Remember and guard against the impacts of the $12 \times 12 \times 12 \times 12$ rule. Instead of judging the speaker for his or her appearance, ancestry, address, accent, or ability to articulate, try instead to understand the speaker. As he or she speaks, try to imagine his or her background and backstory. Visualize the circumstances that might have led him or her to this moment in his or her life.

Practice Self-Awareness

Socrates wrote: "The unexamined life is not worth living." The idea is that if you are not constantly reviewing and examining every aspect of your life to get the best out of it, your life is of little or no value. Thus, a curious paradox thereby arises: to evaluate and judge others less, we must be willing to evaluate and judge our own biases, prejudices, and beliefs more. To replace the natural and instinctive tendency to judge others, we must engage in the continuous and sometimes painful process of scrutinizing and extinguishing our own prejudices.

Artful listeners are always busy examining, reshaping, and reinventing themselves. The outgrowth of this self-awareness fortifies the artful listener's ability to listen without judging; to see things from the speaker's perspective; and to facilitate free-flowing conversation which is good communication.

Tip 4:
Prepare the Environment

In order to create a supportive environment for the conversation, the first step for the artful listener is to examine the conversation site either the day before or early on the day of the conversation. The artful listener inspects the space beforehand in order to modify or eliminate any possible elements or distractions in the environment that may negatively impact the conversation.

Such distractions may include ambient noise, too much or too little light, and space constraints. Other factors to be considered by the artful listener are the availability of food and/or water and the possibility that the conversation may occur during a meal. The artful listener takes into consideration external factors such as the time it takes to reach the site, traffic patterns around the site, and parking conditions.

On the day of the conversation, there are several creative ways to improve the prospects for an artful conversation. In my listening workshops, I create visuals such as taping a note on the entrance door which says, "This is a cell phone free zone, " putting up signs that say "quiet space," or displaying signage with this message: "Use two ears and one mouth." These customized visuals can significantly alter the environment in a positive manner.

There are many ways to welcome the speaker into the conversation space. Here are some of my favorite tips to set the stage for a successful meeting:

- Include the speaker's name on a welcome kiosk;

- Inform the security department of the meeting so that the speaker's name appears on the security clearance list;

- Arrange a special parking space for the speaker and display a sign near the space with the speaker's name on it;

- Assign an "ambassador" to meet the speaker;

- Have a preprinted name badge ready for the speaker; and

- Present the speaker with a welcome gift upon his or her arrival.

As the conversation is about to begin, an artful listener can further facilitate the listening experience by taking these actions: powering off cell phones and computers, asking an assistant to hold all calls during the conversation, and verifying with the speaker if he or she is comfortable (and then taking steps to adjust the environment accordingly).

The listener may also take any number of these situation-specific actions: invite the speaker to move to another space (from standing near a point of entrance to sitting at a conference table); sit side by side with the speaker; offer a bottle of water; ring a little bell or tap a gong; and/or observe a moment of silence.

Tip 5:

Prepare for Distractions

We live in a world of distractions. A distraction is anything that shifts your energy away from your focus. For an artful listener, the focus is on the speaker and the understanding of the message that the speaker intends to convey. The artful listener works hard not to allow distractions to take control of his or her attention and attitude.

To listen artfully, you must completely focus on the speaker and what he or she has to say. In a real sense, you have to make the speaker feel that he or she is the only one in the sometimes crowded room and that there is nowhere else that you would rather be than right there at that very moment.

When you make deliberate and intentional efforts to eliminate the distractions, you communicate to the speaker that you care only about his or her thoughts and nothing else. An emphasis on minimizing distractions to maximize discussions builds trust between you and the speaker because 1) it saves time and energy for the speaker and the listener; 2) the speaker and the listener can approach the conversation with calmness and confidence; and 3) both the speaker and the listener can remain in the zone of free communication for an extended period of time.

All distractions can be classified in one of two categories: those that can be erased and those distractions which should be embraced. Here is another way to put it: distractions can be controlled or are uncontrollable. In either case, where attention goes, energy flows.

Control the Controllables

The infinite power of technology and the ubiquity of digital devices across a myriad of platforms driven by millions of apps and used by billions of people have created an unprecedented level of potential distractions. Never under any circumstances during the conversation should the listener answer a tweet, check email, or react to a notification without seeking respectful permission from the speaker. Such interruptions are controllable, and it is the listener's duty not to react or respond to interruptions of this kind.

To control the controllable, the artful listener approaches the tyranny of distractions armed with the knowledge that some may be eliminated quickly. If the phone rings or a smartphone chimes, the artful listener will say to the speaker, "Excuse me" and turn the phone off. If appropriate, the artful listener may answer the phone and say: "I am in a meeting right now, and I will call you back later."

If there is a knock on a door, the speaker makes the following statement to the person who is knocking: "Excuse me, I am in a meeting now; I will be with you in a few minutes."

Embrace the Uncontrollables

Airplane pilots who encounter "rough air"—a distraction if you will—do not divert from the ultimate destination. Rather, the skilled pilot will seek to avoid (fly over, under, around) the rough air. When the avoidance options are not available, the pilot will take the appropriate measures to keep the passengers safe. Eventually, the plane will enter smoother air.

This is a good way to think about uncontrollable distractions. Such distractions may indeed include weather conditions (rain, lightning, or thunder) as well as sounds of airplanes ascending, ambulances blaring, machines buzzing, children screaming, dogs barking, conference participants talking, etc. Such scenarios may render an artful listener with little or no ability to terminate, mitigate, or eliminate the distraction. In those cases, the best the artful listener can do is to embrace the distractions while maintaining his or her own composure and calm. Here are some ways in which you as the artful listener can manage uncontrollable distractions:

Take a Deep Breath

Although your breathing is an automatic process, you can take control of your breath and take control of where you will focus your attention. According to *Harvard Health Publishing*, deep breathing can be accomplished in this manner: "Find a quiet, comfortable place to sit or lie down. First, take a normal breath. Then try a deep breath: breathe in slowly through your nose, allowing your chest and lower belly to rise as you fill your lungs. Let your abdomen expand fully. Now breathe out slowly through your mouth (or your nose, if that feels more natural)."

This process will result in a calming sensation. Deep breathing has a way of bringing our attention away from distractions back to our breath which is at the center of our being. Because the mind can really only focus on one thing at a time, the focus on breath helps us to return to the here and now—the eternal present.

Trust Your Ears

You are in possession of not one but two amazing listening devices: your ears. In an article entitled "How the Ear Works" on the *University of Maryland Medical Center* website, the ear's normal operation is described in five steps:

1. Sound is transmitted as sound waves from the environment. The sound waves are gathered by the outer ear and sent down the ear canal to the eardrum.

2. The sound waves cause the eardrum to vibrate, which sets the three tiny bones in the middle ear into motion.

3. The motion of the bones causes the fluid in the inner ear or cochlea to move.

4. The movement of the inner ear fluid causes the hair cells in the cochlea to bend. The hair cells change the movement into electrical pulses.

5. These electrical impulses are transmitted to the hearing (auditory) nerve and up to the brain, where they are interpreted as sound.

This means that no matter what the distraction, your ears will continue to process sound efficiently. Do not panic if there is a momentary distraction that you cannot immediately control. Focus on the speaker's words and body language to the exclusion of all else and let your ears do their job.

Recite Positive Listening Affirmations

We listen to ourselves more than we listen to any other person. One way to control the controllables is to exercise control over your thoughts. Control your affirmations, control your thoughts. This will help to create a distraction-free mental zone. Affirmations affect attitudes; attitude affects awareness; and awareness affects your actions.

I recommend that you make this affirmation statement to yourself as often as you can when you prepare for a conversation: "Right now, I am going to clear my mind of distracting thoughts so that I can be fully present for the speaker during the next 15 minutes." Your affirmation will have a profound effect on how you focus, concentrate, and listen to another speaker. Furthermore, these regular recitations of the affirmation statements will put you in the right mindset at the outset of artful conversations. Such statements will harness your awareness, focus your attention, and allow you to concentrate on the positive energy of the speaker and what he or she wants to say. Here are some additional examples of affirmation statements:

"Be swift to listen, slow to speak."

"Listen first, think second."

"Maintain an open mind and a closed mouth."

"Seek first to understand then to be understood."

Tip 6:
Arrive at the
Conversation Site Early

Even though you may have visited the site the day before, it is to your advantage to show up early on the day of the actual conversation. You will want to make sure that you allow plenty of time for driving to the site and parking your car which may be a challenge in some downtown areas.

Once you are in the room where the conversation will take place, you may have the opportunity to put up signage, arrange the tables and chairs in the room to your liking, and adjust the temperature. Arriving early also gives you the opportunity to finish consuming any breakfast or lunch items that may be offered in the room (as in a convention setting) as well as drinks such as coffee or juice. If your speaker arrives and desires to eat during the conversation, you will show courtesy to the speaker by choosing something light like a roll while the speaker eats.

After you have eaten, it is time to visit the restroom and check your appearance one last time. When you return to the conversation site and wait for your speaker to arrive, check your email and text messages to see if you have any communication from the speaker concerning your meeting. About five minutes before the appointed meeting time, close your computer and turn off your cell phone. Spend the last moments reviewing any notes that you may have regarding the meeting. If you are so inclined, practice deep breathing while reviewing the notes. Take comfort in knowing that you have done everything in your power to prepare yourself and the environment for a successful conversation. You are now ready to conduct an artful conversation.

Part II:

DURING THE CONVERSATION

At its core, artful listening is communication. The objective of artful listening is to communicate by receiving and transmitting meanings from many sources—internal and external, verbal and nonverbal, physical and metaphysical, secular and spiritual.

The painter uses his or her inspiration and brush, paint, canvas, and light to bring that inspiration into reality for generations to experience. The pianist uses his or her inspiration through hands, keys, notes, and silence to produce music that may move millions. The planter uses the seed, the sun, the soil, and his or her strength to render a life-giving harvest. The artful listener uses not just the ears but his or her eyes, mouth, face, and body to facilitate an authentic conversation which can be life changing for the speaker and listener. By combining the physical (conversation) and the metaphysical (connection), the artful listener, like any other artist, creates the sensational (community) and the spiritual (communication). Let us examine how such a work of listening art might be fashioned.

Tip 7:
Introduce Yourself

First of all, remember that your greeting reflects the amount of time and effort that you have put into preparation for the conversation. As an artful listener, you should feel confident when you have done everything possible to enhance the environment for the conversation. Though some preparations such as getting enough sleep are "below the waterline" of the conversation, these steps have a way of showing themselves during the conversation, and the speaker will sense your confidence and strength.

With regard to handshakes, the COVID-19 world is adjusting to a different reality in which physical greetings and farewells will not be so physical. In the virus-conscious environment where we live today, physical touching (especially with a stranger) has become socially unacceptable. What will replace it? We suggest the following three ways: bowing slightly, nodding the head, and touching the heart.

Bowing slightly indicates reverence in many cultures and is growing to be an acceptable form of nonverbal greeting and farewell in the post-virus world. Nodding the head also conveys respect without any physical touching. Our third suggested way of bidding farewell, putting your right hand to your heart for a few seconds, acts as a powerful sign of the sacred connection that the listener feels with the speaker.

Practice these gestures and discover the gesture that feels most comfortable for you. You may also find that some combination of these gestures may be perfect for your own personal sense of style. For more information on the trends in nonverbal welcoming gestures, see "6 Ways People around the World Say Hello—without Touching" by Sunny Fitzgerald available at www.nationalgeographic.com/travel/2020/03/ways-people-around-world-say-hello-without-touching-coronavirus/.

If you do not know the name of the speaker prior to the conversation, I recommend that you listen very carefully for the speaker's name choice during the introduction. Magdalene Shepherd may say, "Magdalene Shepherd, but call me Maggie," or Robert Baker may say, "Robert Baker, but call me Bob." If this occurs, use the preferred name of the speaker throughout the conversation. Remembering the preferred name is your first step in building trust with the speaker. If you do not happen to capture the name during the greeting, it is perfectly acceptable to ask the speaker politely to repeat it.

Remember that the speaker loves to hear his or her name, so be sure to memorize it and use the preferred name frequently during the conversation. To forget or to not use the name of the speaker will seriously damage the trust that you are seeking to build during the course of the whole conversation.

Obtaining the business card from the speaker is also a must for the listener. If the speaker provides you with a business card at the time of the greeting, receive it with two hands. Read the business card quickly, noting the speaker's name and title. Then thank the speaker for giving you the business card. Tap it gracefully and place it in the pocket of your shirt or jacket closest to the heart.

A handshake has been traditionally linked to transparency, openness, genuineness, and trust. If a handshake is acceptable to the speaker, it should last no longer than it takes to exchange the words of introduction. Any greeting that you choose should be accompanied with a smile and eye contact with the speaker. Even if the speaker is the chief executive officer of your company or the person interviewing you for a job, try to think of him or her during the introduction as an old friend that you have not seen in some time.

Tip 8:
Welcome the Speaker

It has been my experience that rushed conversations never go well. When the speaker is already glancing at his or her watch and contemplating the next meeting, the chances for an authentic conversation in that space are virtually nil. As previously discussed, you should make every effort to reach out to the speaker in advance of the conversation to discuss the subject, date, time, location, and duration. Having an agreed-upon duration lessens the chances of a rushed conversation.

Moving from a standing position to a sitting position has many benefits. First of all, the change will minimize any possible height differences between the listener and the speaker. For example, the speaker may be a young adult, someone who is physically challenged, or a senior citizen. Sitting together dismantles this potential barrier to communication and will allow both the speaker and listener to participate fully in the conversation.

Sitting together also has a powerful psychological effect. In the Native American tradition of holding meetings, all participants sit on the ground in a circle. Everyone is able to see everyone else on an equal basis. This represents a powerful way to level the playing (conversing) field; the phrase "on common ground" becomes literally true.

To facilitate the change from standing to sitting, I recommend that you arrive early at the place where the conversation will occur. At that time, establish a space where both you and the speaker can be seated comfortably. After the introductions have been completed, politely ask the speaker to be seated in the space that you have already prepared. If appropriate to the situation, you may offer the speaker a bottle of water or a soft drink. This may also be a moment when you can engage in social conversation with the speaker. For example, you may ask him or her about his or her journey to the meeting space.

You will discover quickly whether the speaker is in the proper frame of mind for such talk or whether he or she is ready to go directly into the conversation. Always be open to listening and learning more about the speaker in these moments before the formal conversation commences.

Tip 9:

Take a Position near the Speaker

Sitting face to face with the speaker may seem to be confrontational and more like an interrogation than a conversation. A position just to the right of the speaker usually aligns more comfortably with the speaker's preferences and also presents several benefits for the listener.

For example, most people are right handed, and certain cultures put priority on the right hand. In an article entitled "How to Get on the Boss's Good Side—Literally," Carol Kinsey Goman noted that "a series of recent studies by Daniel Casasanto, a psychologist at the New School for Social Research, show that we associate our dominant side with good and our nondominate side with bad, preferring products and people that happen to be on our 'good' side."

In addition, there is research that suggests that our two ears process sounds differently. Don Glass stated this phenomenon in this manner: "The left hemisphere of the brain dominates over the right in processing different sounds. Specifically, the left hemisphere dominates in processing rapidly changing sounds such as in speech, and the right hemisphere dominates in processing prolonged tones such as in music. However, the processing of sound actually begins in our ears, before sound reaches the brain. Because the right ear connects to the brain's left hemisphere, it's the dominant ear for processing rapidly changing sounds, and vice versa, the left ear dominates in processing prolonged tones." We may extrapolate from this information that listening with the left ear is advantageous when the listener is engaged in a conversation.

In a scientific article entitled "Laterality of Basic Auditory Perception," Yvonne S. Sininger and Anjali Bhatara discussed the differences in ear function this way: "The LEA (Left Ear Advantage) for tonal stimuli is felt to be due to more direct connections between the left ear and the right auditory cortex which has been shown to be primary for spectral analysis and tonal processing." This means that your left ear may be the preferable ear to use in processing the analytical information that is shared when conversing.

However, be prepared to move to the left of the speaker if he or she requests that you do so. The speaker's comfort should always be the listener's No. 1 priority.

Tip 10:
Memorialize the Conversation

It is very important for the listener to receive permission from the speaker to take notes or record the conversation. If the speaker grants you such permission, you may either use a pen and pad or a recording device.

The pen and pad that you use should be chosen thoughtfully. Using a pen with the name of the speaker's company or school printed on it can send a positive signal of connection between you and the speaker.

If there is no such pen available, I recommend purchasing a pen that helps to project your professional image. One of the most respected pen companies in the world is Montblanc™. Its pens are known for their stylish design and craftsmanship; they are often used as prizes in sales contests and other corporate competitions. Using a Montblanc™ or other high-end pen sends a message to the speaker that you are a serious professional ready for an authentic conversation.

For your pad, I recommend a portfolio-type leather folder that has a space for your pen, business cards, and other documents such as resumes and writing samples. A portfolio in a dark color that zips all the way around is both secure and attractive. Such folders cost about fifty dollars and can be purchased at office supply stores and stationery shops.

If you desire to memorialize the conversation by using a recording device, please be aware that you must obtain permission from the speaker before using the device. Taping a conversation without the permission of the speaker is illegal in certain jurisdictions and should be avoided at all costs.

Once you obtain the speaker's permission, display the recording device in full view of the speaker and turn on the device. At the beginning of the recording, clearly state the following: your name and the speaker's name as well as the date, city, and state where the conversation is taking place. Once the conversation begins, do not touch or check the device because interacting with the device in any way will create an unnecessary distraction.

Used carefully, a recording device can be a very effective way of memorializing conversations conducted in connection with oral history projects. In addition, journalists frequently use recording devices when they want to capture the exact words of the speaker for short news stories or for longer, in-depth profiles.

Note that if you are not recording with a cell phone, I recommend that you switch your cell phone to the Silent or Do Not Disturb mode and put the phone out of sight so as not to detract from the conversation. Research has repeatedly shown that the mere presence of a cell phone while two individuals are in conversation deteriorates the quantity and quality of the conversation (even if the cell phone is turned off). The listener in a conversation who has a cell phone in plain sight is sending a subtle message that a possible cell phone interaction (by voice call, text, or alert) is more important than the current conversation. The speaker may perceive this and feel devalued. If this happens, the speaker may also devalue the conversation itself.

Tip 11:

Use Appropriate Body Language

A significant part of an artful conversation is nonverbal. Along with words, we send messages through body language. Here are some tips on how the listener can use body language to demonstrate his or her deep commitment to understanding the speaker in an artful way:

Maintain Eye Contact throughout the Conversation

The more that you maintain your eye contact with the speaker, the more you demonstrate your attentionality, civility, respect, honor, and concern. You are truly "paying attention" to what the speaker is saying. If the eyes are the window of the soul, then maintaining eye contact will help to bring the souls of the speaker and listener into harmony and transcendence.

Eye contact lets the speaker and the listener know they are visible to each other. Such visibility imparts value, respect, humanity, and compassion. Interestingly, in South Africa, a common salutary greeting for "hello" among Zulus is "Sawubona," which means "I see you." The typical response is "Shiboka," meaning "I exist for you."

An artful listener listens with his or her eyes. At the same time, eye contact communicates these thoughts to the speaker: "I see you. I hear you. I value you. What you have to say is important to me. I exist to hear, listen, understand, and respond to you."

When two people engage in conversation, a conversational bond forms between them. The story, the narrative, and the experience bind the listener to the speaker and vice versa. The speaker-listener bond has the potential to transform the shared experience and create something altogether new. The relationship can progress from eye contact to heart contact, conversation to connection, rapport to relationship, and talk to trust.

When conversing with a person who has sight loss, do not assume that the individual has no sight at all. Maintain respect and find creative and imaginative ways to let the person know that you see him or her, that he or she is visible to you, and that his or her diminished sight does not make them invisible. Humans have the gift of echolocation which is defined as "the location of objects by reflected sounds"; it is known that sound waves create images in the brain. Blind people dream, visualize, and see with their minds' eye. When conversing with a visually challenged speaker, I recommend that you continue to look at him or her directly throughout the conversation and always verbalize your own physical actions to him or her ("I will move over closer to you in order to hear you better"). In a group conversation, remember to address the visually challenged speaker directly by using his or her own name.

In the United States, eye contact communicates confidence, credibility, and connection. In Arab countries, people use prolonged eye contact to gauge trustworthiness; the more eye contact that is made by a person, the more trustworthy that person is considered to be. However, in Asian, African, and Latin American cultures, only intermittent eye contact is deemed acceptable. It is worthwhile to enhance one's multicultural competence concerning eye contact to ensure that you are always showing the utmost respect to speakers from different cultures.

Looking around during a conversation sends a signal to the speaker that you are not entirely focused and interested in what he or she has to say. Such eye movements will damage or destroy the free flow of an authentic conversation. A pleasant gaze of interest and curiosity should be what supports and enlivens the interaction of listener and speaker from beginning to end.

Be Still
One of the best ways to listen is to be silent, and one of the

best ways to be silent is to be physically still. The listener should become comfortable with the silent patches of time that occur when the speaker reaches for a new thought, ponders an idea, or seeks to articulate a point.

Sitting still sends the signal that you value what a person has to say to such a degree that you want to immerse yourself in his or her words.

Lean Slightly toward the Speaker to Show Your Attentiveness

Poet and philosopher Mark Nepo wrote: "To listen is to lean in, softly, with a willingness to be changed by what you hear." Leaning in is a physical representation of the gift of attention. A popular exercise that I use in my workshops is called: "Be where your feet are." In this simple but powerful activity, I encourage seated participants to plant both feet on the floor. They are asked to feel the floor and sense their toes rooted to the ground. From there I encourage participants to feel their feet, ankles, legs, thighs, waist, abdomen, chest, shoulders, neck, and head. The exercise points out the importance of "showing up" and being present in the present.

When your attention goes to the speaker, your energy will flow to the speaker. Like the branches of the Guanacaste tree literally leaning to receive the resplendent rays of the sun, a listener should lean in and receive the radiant remarks of the speaker in a quest to achieve common understanding. As the maxim goes, "To hear you must be fully here."

Leaning in is not just a physical gesture; it is also a psychological and spiritual movement. It means that you are investing in what the speaker has to say in your own mind and spirit. Leaning in lets the speaker know that you wish to optimize the opportunity for rich connection, maximize the magic of the moment, and prioritize the perspectives and point of view of the speaker. Leaning in is listening in.

There is a proper posture for achieving mastery of just about any sports activity. This is especially true for the martial arts. The correct posture in karate, judo, or Taekwondo contributes to proper blocks and strikes. If the posture is poor, the performance is poor; the martial artist is more easily knocked off balance or moves with decreased speed. The same is true for the art of listening. Sit upright and then lean in slightly forward toward the speaker. You are now in a posture for a winsome conversation.

Avoid the Pitfalls of Inappropriate Body Language

Remember that the speaker is consciously and subconsciously interpreting your body language during the conversation. He or she will receive a great deal of information from you over and above your words. The speaker may detect enthusiasm, boredom, or irritation very quickly in the expression around your eyes, the set of your jaw, and the slope of your shoulders. An overly relaxed posture can indicate that the listener is not really interested in what the speaker has to say. Crossed arms and legs and fingers send a message of resistance that the speaker will quickly perceive. Once that happens, the authentic conversation that you have so assiduously created will be in grave danger of falling apart.

Tip 12:
Listen Carefully

During my years of teaching at the collegiate level, I have created a series of tried and true strategies designed to help students capture and retain the message of a speaker.

I call it the Listening Sixers: Repeat, Restate, Rephrase, Rest, Recap, Redo. In this section, I will delineate each strategy as well as discuss the Six Day Week, a recommended way of practicing these powerful reflective techniques.

Repeat

Paying attention to a word that the speaker uses more than once and then repeating it back to him or her is a great listening strategy. It lets the speaker know you are tracking his or her thoughts and making a genuine effort to understand them. In the business world, there are several important words that are repeated by executives and managers frequently. Here are three examples: "changes," "costs," and "schedules." When you hear one of these words in a business conversation, that word and topic are likely to become significant parts of that conversation.

Restate

Restating a few words or a phrase of the speaker confirms to the speaker that he or she is being heard. You show that you are in step with the speaker's language. The restatement will also help you clarify your own understanding of the speaker's thoughts. For example, after the speaker, a prospective purchaser of a car, has talked about his or her requirements for a new vehicle, you may restate those requirements in this manner: "I understand that you are looking for a small, used SUV with low mileage."

Rephrase

In the rephrase part of the Listening Sixers process, recast what you have heard from the speaker in your own words to clarify your understanding through the speaker's confirmation. You may do this using "I" statements such as the following:

- "What I heard you say was . . . Correct?"

- "As I understand what you have shared, your thoughts are . . . Is that it?"

- "Based on what I have been hearing, you said . . . Did I hear you correctly?"

When you use restatements such as these, you empower the speaker to confirm or clarify his or her thoughts. In response, the speaker may either agree ("Yes, that is what I meant to say") or clarify his or her position ("Well, what I really meant was …").

Rephrasing takes effort because you are taking what the speaker has offered and then reshaping it based on what you understood from the speaker's point of view. This hard work is the artwork of artful listening. The process involves more than repeating the speaker's words. You are reframing the speaker's thoughts in such a way that your own takeaway is understandable to the speaker. Be sure to paraphrase at this point and not simply repeat the speaker's words. Instead, articulate your understanding with your own words by including an "I" in your statement as noted above.

Rest

Take a pause for the cause. Active listening is hard work, and listening, too, requires active rest. This pause may last from several seconds up to a minute. Making the deliberate and conscious decision to pause is in itself a kind of feedback. If you are taking the cue from the speaker or using the pause to collect your thoughts, by resting you are offering a subtle signal to the speaker that you are listening and assimilating his or her thoughts.

Recap

With this Sixer strategy, your aim is to recapitulate the speaker's message so well that you receive affirmation from the speaker. After hearing your recap, the speaker will indicate confirmatory affirmation with words or phrases like "yes," "that's right," "exactly," "spot on," and "correct." Your ability to synthesize major points, storylines, and patterns informs the speaker that you have listened well and that you have retained what the speaker has shared. A key aspect of artful listening is that you can recap accurately what is shared. When you recap, you give implicit feedback: you show the speaker that you listened. Just as importantly, you demonstrate to yourself that you have listened.

Here is an example of a good recap by an artful listener about a conversation with a potential buyer concerning the purchase of a car: "You shared that you need to replace your Chevy sedan and purchase a late model Toyota or Honda this week if the price is less than $30,000. Is that a fair summary of what we discussed?"

Redo

Artful listening is about perceiving each conversation as an opportunity to build good listening habits.

The most important tip that I can share with you is to practice, practice, practice. Start to apply the Listening Sixers in your conversations with family members, friends, employees, colleagues, and supervisors.

Why not practice the Listening Sixers over the course of this coming week? I recommend that you practice one technique each day for six days. Here's a sample schedule:

Day 1 (Repeat): Engage in a conversation. Pick out a key word repeated by the speaker. Practice repeating the speaker's key word at an appropriate time during the conversation such as after an interruption or during a pause by the speaker.

Day 2 (Restate): Listen carefully during a conversation today. Pick out a key phrase by the speaker. Practice restating that speaker's key phrase during the conversation.

Day 3 (Rephrase): Engage in a conversation on this day. Pick out a key statement by the speaker. Practice rephrasing the statement in your own words and then state it at an appropriate time during the conversation. This process will boost your listening skills and confidence.

Day 4 (Rest): Listen artfully during a conversation on this day. Pick out a key word, phrase, or statement by the speaker. When the speaker pauses, you should rest and reflect on the word, phrase, or statement that you have chosen.

Day 5 (Recap): Engage in an artful conversation today. Pick out key words, phrases, or statements by the speaker. At the end of the conversation, summarize the conversation by recapitulating what you have heard from the perspective of the speaker.

Day 6 (Redo): It's time to review the week's conversations. How did you do with regard to the Listening Sixers? What type of feedback did you gain from the speakers during the experience? What ways might you improve? Use the answers to these questions as a basis for utilizing the Listening Sixers in the future to improve and refine your listening skills.

Tip 13:
Do Not Be Afraid of
Pauses or Lulls

The legendary jazz trumpeter Miles Davis said: "Don't play what's there; play what's not there." This is a new type of listening where we not only hear what's there (the words) but also what's not there (the wonders waiting within the silences of the words).

The silence is a pause, and there is a purpose for every pause just as there is a reason for every remark. As the management guru Peter Drucker noted: "The most important thing in communication is hearing what isn't said." Rather than avoiding pauses, the artful listener accepts, affirms, and acknowledges them. The artful listener listens to the speaker holistically: the speaker's points, perspectives, and pauses.

When you artfully listen, you recognize and appreciate the beauty of pauses. Consider the resplendent rhythm and beauty of the beating heart. The heart does not beat, beat, beat. Rather, the heart beats and pauses, beats and pauses. A person talks and pauses, talks and pauses. Pauses are a natural part of talking and therefore listening. Prepare yourself to listen to them.

Consider the following sentence: iwillbeheretolisten. Consider it again: I-W-I-L-L-B-E-H-E-R-E-T-O-L-I-S-T-E-N. What is missing in both accounts? Pauses (spaces) between the letters and words. Consider the second sentence again with inserted pauses/spaces: I WILL BE HERE TO LISTEN. The importance of the spaces points up the importance of pauses in communication. Listening is a cocreative, cogenerative process, and the listener must listen to how the speaker selects pauses, spaces, and gaps in the conversation to craft his or her message. To disregard the pause is to potentially misunderstand the speaker's intended message.

To comprehend the power of the pause, think of the difficulty of listening to a speaker at a noisy restaurant. Plates are clinking, conversations are going, music is blaring, and orders are being taken. Listening to a speaker when there is so much noise is nearly impossible. Why? Because of the constant bombardment of sound—no silent spaces. What would be otherwise intelligible speech and discernible sound is a muddled mix of meaningless messages because there are no pauses.

Much like a miner panning for gold, the artful listener meticulously combs the conversation listening for the speaker's nuggets of wisdom imbedded in the pauses in his or her story. Every person—every speaker—has a gold mine between his or her ears. The context (pauses) can be just as rich in content as the words conveyed. When the listener allows, acknowledges, and accepts well-placed pauses, the most charming and informative conversations inevitably come about. Here are my top tips and takeaways concerning pauses or lulls during a conversation:

Know the Cause of the Pause

The diversity of pauses allows the speaker and listener to cooperatively convey their ideas fully. The artful listener masters understanding of the different types of pauses in order to amplify the listening experience. As with many tips and techniques about artful listening presented in this book, the key is to experience the pause from the standpoint of the speaker in order to assess how the pause is intended to be used and understood.

The speaker may use a pause to emphasize certain information, allow time to process what has been presented, or enhance the message delivery. At the same time, the pause can build suspense and create interest and curiosity.

Be Not Distracted by Pauses

The artful listener is not distracted by pauses but attracted to them. Do not be distracted by unintentional pauses such as the speaker's filler words in a conversation ("uhs," "ers," and "ums") which may signal that the speaker is not yet finished speaking or is selecting the right phraseology. The artful listener is aware that people from different cultures, backgrounds, and ethnicities have different filler sounds.

Pause with the Speaker

A pause is not the opportunity to commandeer the conversation, inject your inimitable intelligence, suggest your solution to the speaker's problem, or boast of your brilliance. It is an opportunity to continue to cocreate the message with the speaker. Think of a speaker's pause as a timely opportunity for the listener to mentally verify and/or sum up what the speaker has said. If you are waiting for a pause so that you can jump in quickly with your own agenda, then you are neither artfully nor actively listening.

Let the Speaker Pause

By respecting the pause, you as the listener show respect to the speaker. Allow him or her to pause in his or her unique way without judging the pause or the producer of the pause. When you acknowledge that the pause is the speaker's own, you show immense respect to him or her, and you allow the wonders waiting within the silences to manifest themselves. In the spirit of Miles Davis, you allow the speaker to play—and yourself to learn—the musical notes that are not there.

Tip 14:
Never Interrupt the Speaker

As we have noted often in this book, artful listening depends on creating a free flow of communication between the speaker and the listener. Carl R. Rogers noted: "Good communication, or free communication, within or between people is always therapeutic."

Interrupting the speaker interferes with the goal of good communication. Furthermore, it is an especially egregious way of violating this core principle of artful listening. It disrupts the flow of the conversation, damages the trust between the speaker and the listener, and jeopardizes the entire relationship between the two. How?

First, interruptions are extremely disruptive to the conversational flow. When we interrupt, instead of having a listener, a speaker, and a conversation, we have two speakers and no more conversation. Interruptions upend the entire process.

Second, the tendency to interrupt a speaker with questions early and often prevents the speaker from ever communicating his or her points. Even if the speaker recovers from the derailments caused by interruptions, the subsequent points the speaker makes may be vastly different from the points that the speaker formulated before the conversation ever began.

Third, interrupting might have the impact of causing the speaker to forget what he or she was preparing to say or already saying. It has probably happened to every one of us. You lost your train of thought when you were interrupted. Conversely, at some point in the past, you interrupted a speaker and then apologized to him or her which probably made the situation even worse. Such a conversation might be partially salvaged by the listener who may remind the speaker of his or her train of thought preceding the interruption, but the damage is done.

Finally, interruptions negatively affect the speaker on an emotional level and destroy whatever trust exists between the speaker and the listener. Even the speaker who recovers from an interruption will have diminished enthusiasm for the rest of the conversation. Hence, to interrupt is to negatively impact the speaker's positive feelings toward the listener.

Remember that a speaker's thoughts are extensions of the speaker. Indeed, it is the person, not just his or her prose, position, perspective, or point of view that we want to understand.

To interrupt his or her thoughts is to risk upending the speaker emotionally. Not only does it hinder the communicative act, but also it blocks the opportunity for you to connect with the person who is speaking. This much is also obvious. The *less* you interrupt, the more you have the opportunity to connect with what the speaker is saying; to connect with the speaker's overall message; and to connect with the speaker himself or herself.

The word "jeopardy" is defined as "danger of loss, harm, or failure." The game play during the television show *Jeopardy* helps to illustrate the importance of not interrupting. To gain dollar amounts, contestants must listen very carefully to the clue and respond in the form of a question. To be eligible to respond, one of the three contestants must press a handheld device to "ring in" before the other two players. At times, contestants will ring in too soon without carefully listening to the clue or thinking through their response. Whether out of nervousness or competitiveness, they are penalized for this type of interruption and jeopardize their chances of winning money.

In business, interruptions may jeopardize your potential for retaining and/or keeping your employment. Interrupting the person who is interviewing you for a job may result in a quick and unpleasant rejection. Interrupting the chief executive officer of your company during his or her answer to a shareholder at the annual shareholders meeting may have similar adverse consequences. No matter how well intended your reason for interrupting, the potential impact of the interruption may be difficult or impossible for you to undo.

Therefore, keep two things in mind with regard to interruptions. First, the decision *not* to interrupt is always entirely within your control. Secondly, interruption by the listener equals eruption by the speaker.

Tip 15:
Let the Speaker Finish
His or Her Thoughts

Think of how good it feels to conclude an important or difficult task—to finish, for example, your first marathon, to put the final brush stroke on a portrait, or to write the last sentence of the bar exam.

We know from science that this feeling is physiological. According to Jennifer Berry, "Endorphins are chemicals produced naturally by the nervous system to cope with pain or stress. They are often called 'feel-good' chemicals because they can act as a pain reliever and happiness booster."

During an authentic conversation, the speaker is actually reacting to the situation not only intellectually but physically. To put it another way, being heard, listened to, and understood by an artful listener feels great. Indeed, Carl R. Rogers, the famed psychologist who first formulated the concept of active listening, emphasized this point when he wrote: "When someone really hears you without passing judgment on you, without trying to take responsibility for you, without trying to mold you, it feels damn good."

What does feeling good have to do with allowing the speaker to finish? Everything. Whenever the speaker has the opportunity to select the right phrase, put forth an aptly selected idea, present a thought in just the way intended, or bring an idea to its conclusion, the speaker is "finishing" not only a thought but the creative process. When the speaker has completed the act and the art involved in articulating and expressing his or her ideas, he or she has, in a real sense, "finished" a masterpiece.

The speaker's reward for the successful completion of his or her thoughts is a release of endorphins and a feeling sometimes called a "runner's high." The speaker experiences the same intoxicating feeling as do artists, builders, composers, designers, and writers when they finish their works of art. This is why it is so important to allow the speakers to complete their stories.

How can the listener make sure to always let the speaker finish? First, the speaker should not assume that he or she knows the speaker's thoughts before these ideas are completely articulated. This assumption is one of the biggest blocks to letting the speaker finish. One important reason why listeners think they can predict or finish a person's thoughts is due to what is called the speech/understanding differential.

While the typical speaker will talk at a rate of about 125 words per minute, the human mind can process approximately 400 spoken words per minute. This difference between the speed of a speaker's spoken words and the processing speed of a listener's mind is a gap that will always exist in conversation. On the basis of this gap, the untrained listener often assumes that he or she can read the speaker's mind and predict the final course of the speaker's thought processes. Instead, the astute listener should take note of this space, optimize the differential to its artful extent, and allow the speaker to have the mental and physical satisfaction of finishing his or her comments.

What should the listener do with the gap time? Use it to review what the speaker is saying, reflect on how the speaker is saying it, and recap your understanding of what the speaker has shared. To interrupt the speaker during the gap time because you as the listener can process words faster than the speaker can talk (but you the listener cannot control your urge to interrupt) may be perceived by the speaker as embarrassing and rude. Don't do it.

Try something new. In grade school we were taught the three steps to use when coming to potentially dangerous places such as street corners and railroad crossings: stop, look, and listen. The steps are designed to protect the safety of all concerned. Essentially, we were taught to *stop* (quit playing, running, walking, or talking), *look* (focus our attention on the cars, street, trains, and tracks) and *listen* (for the sounds of oncoming cars or trains or the words of police officers, parents, or other adults).

Stop, look, and listen were lifesavers back then. These steps are also conversational lifesavers today. They have the power and potential to bring unnecessary listening activities to a standstill, focus the listener's attention on the speaker's priorities, and dispose the listener to greater awareness of what the speaker has to share. We must *stop* focusing on distractions and interruptions; *look* at the speaker with focus and attention; and *listen* with curiosity and interest to every one of the speaker's words.

Just as a young child should not cross the railroad tracks before the signal goes up, an artful listener should not jump in prematurely when the speaker is still talking. Instead, show reverence to the one who speaks. You do so by letting the speaker finish. Only then may you finish listening.

Tip 16:

Provide Feedback to the Speaker

In the field of communication, the traditional cycle includes two parties—the sender (speaker) and the receiver (listener). The speaker sends a message. The listener receives the message. The listener interprets the message and sends feedback to the speaker to confirm that the listener understood the message. The speaker reacts to the feedback by providing the listener with confirmation (that the speaker was understood) and/or clarification (of what was not understood). From there, the process continues again.

What is crucial to the process is how the speaker and the listener cocreate the message. The feedback that the listener provides to the speaker has a major role in facilitating the message that the speaker is attempting to convey. The listener's feedback manifests itself in three major ways:

1. Understanding (The listener utilizes phrases such as "yes," "I understand," and "I see" during the conversation.)

2. Clarifying (The listener asks questions during the conversation such as "And what happened next?" and/or makes statements such as "You mentioned you were surprised, please, continue …" to improve his or her understanding of the speaker's line of thinking.)

3. Summarizing (The listener provides thoughtful feedback at the end of the conversation to recapitulate understanding: "Let me recap what I have heard, and you let me know if I am on point.")

Consistent with the traditional communication cycle, providing feedback to the speaker is therefore a continuous process with the listener understanding and clarifying during the conversation and summarizing at the end of the conversation.

1. **Understanding** (The listener utilizes phrases such as "yes," "I understand," and "I see" during the conversation.)

   William James wrote: "The deepest principle in human nature is the craving to be appreciated." The artful listener knows the speaker is looking for engagement throughout the course of the conversation. The artful listener uses feedback phrases such as "yes," "I understand," and "I see" which lets the speaker know that "I'm following, I'm with you, you are being heard, I appreciate your thoughts." Notice that using these phrases does not mean that the listener accepts, assents, approves, or agrees with the speaker's arguments. Instead, the listener's use of such phrases indicates to the speaker that the listener is following the trajectory of the conversation from the speaker's point of view.

   While understanding does not mean agreement, it means something far more valuable to the listener-speaker relationship: the intention to accept the speaker, the effort to attune to the speaker's wavelength, and the good faith to attain the speaker's point of view. These three aspirations facilitate trust and help the listener build an emotional connection with the speaker necessary for an authentic conversation.

2. **Clarifying** (The listener asks questions during the conversation such as "And what happened next?" and/or makes statements such as "You mentioned you were surprised, please, continue …" to improve his or her understanding of the speaker's line of thinking.)

   In the course of conversation, the speaker and the listener are involved in cocreating art. It is reasonable to assume that the art may manifest itself fully only in the crucible of the conversation itself. Simply put, the speaker himself or herself might not know the complete scope and shape of his or her thought until presented with an unfettered opportunity to voice it. That is what the listener's questions are designed to do: create within the speaker a deeper sense of awareness, cognizance, or insight that gently nudges the *speaker* to discover more fully what he or she is trying to say.

When the listener's questions are met with responses from the speaker such as "Yes, that is what I meant" or "No, that is not exactly it," the listener is gaining instant feedback which either confirms the message sent by the speaker or indicates that the message needs to be refined.

Each question should have a direct connection to something the speaker has said. Here is an example from the model conversation that appears at the end of this section:

> CEO (William): "OK. After the ski season is over, the pool will be closed for resurfacing and painting. It will take about a month. The front desk will be open from 9 a.m. to 9 p.m. during the week but 24 hours a day on Saturday and Sunday for check-ins and check-outs. The shuttle bus service from the resort to the town of Steamboat Springs will be changed to Saturday and Sunday only. Have you got that?"
>
> COPYWRITER (Reginald): "Yes, sir. Should I check with the front desk manager at the resort to verify the exact dates for the changes?"
>
> CEO (William): "That's all right with me."

Reginald recognizes the dates for the changes as crucial to the message. His question artfully directs William's attention to the need to verify the exact dates for the changes. With William's assent to Reginald's request to check with the front desk manager, Reginald has effectively allowed *William* to discover that his own message needed to include the schedule for the changes.

This is why it is so important to ask questions during the conversation that are germane to what the speaker has said. In effect, a transformation takes place: the listener becomes the speaker, and the speaker becomes the listener. Just as the listener helps the speaker create the thoughts, the speaker (in receiving the feedback from the listener) helps the listener create or confirm understanding. In this case, the message itself is changed by the question. Here are several important tips to help you formulate your questions during a conversation:

- Pause before and after you ask a question. Once you ask the question, give the speaker sufficient time to articulate an answer.

- Do not rush the speaker. Be patient. Avoid saying "yeah, yeah, yeah" or "OK, OK, OK" or "got it, got it, got it"; these repetitive phrases in rapid fire have a way of hurrying the speaker and compromising the quality of the conversation.

- Ask questions sincerely and without rancor. Blunt, harsh, and/or intimidating questions will damage the trust between the listener and the speaker and may result in the premature end and ultimate failure of the conversation.

- Do not answer your own questions. Ask a question and then give the speaker the opportunity to finish.

- Ask one question at a time. Be careful not to ask two or more questions at one time within a single query. Such questions may confuse the speaker. Here is an example: "Would you like to buy the blue car with leather seats and accept $5,000 for your trade in?"

- Avoid the why-based questions which may seem accusatory. Why-based questions provoke defensiveness in the hearer. An open-ended inquiry is more authentic and will be more effective because it helps garner feedback from the speaker's perspective. Here is an example:

> Accusatory question: "Why would you want a used car if you can get a new one for the same price?"
>
> Open-ended question: "If you had the opportunity to have a new car for about the same money as a used car, how might that option appeal to you?"

- Avoid the closed-ended questions that result in "yes" and "no" answers which actually may choke off communication. Open-ended questions invite the speaker to answer from his or her perspective and offer the opportunity to respond more fully. On the flip side, open-ended questions allow the listener, in turn, to be able to listen to the speaker more fully. Here is an example of a closed-ended question and how it could be recast as a more open-ended one:

> Closed-ended question: "Would you like to pur-
> chase this car today?"
>
> Open-ended question: "Do you have any other
> thoughts about becoming the owner of this car
> today?"

- Be careful to avoid leading questions which can be con-
strued as insulting or rude. Here are two examples: "Are
you still driving that old car?" or "Wouldn't you prefer the
condo by the lake rather than the one near the beach?" Such
questions show more about the listener's agendas than the
speaker's needs. Such questions reveal that the listener is
not listening from the point of view of the speaker but from
the listener's own perspective.

3. **Summarizing** (The listener provides thoughtful feedback at
the end of the conversation to recapitulate understanding: "Let
me recap what I have heard, and you let me know if I am on
point.")

Once the speaker finishes, the conversation has not ended.
Rather, the juncture is an opportunity to let the speaker know
he or she has been heard. In his book *The 7 Habits of Highly
Effective People*, Stephen Covey noted: "The biggest communication problem is we do not listen to understand. We listen to
reply." The listener's ability to summarize is an important form
of feedback that shows he or she was listening to understand
the speaker and not merely biding time until his or her turn
to speak. In addition, the summary builds trust, confirms understanding, minimizes misunderstanding, and demonstrates

willingness to not only understand the message but also the messenger.

In the model conversation that appears at the end of this section, the summary statement by Reginald Salisbury and the affirmation of that statement by William Brooks are good examples of the interaction of the listener and speaker at the end of a conversation. This exchange is as follows:

> COPYWRITER (Reginald)
> (to William): "Yes, sir. To recap, in the article for the newsletter about the Steamboat resort, I will include the pool being closed, the front desk hours being changed, the shuttle schedule being revised, and the special assessment being planned for next year. Is that it so far?"
>
> CEO (William)
> (to Reginald): "Yes. So far."

Much like cellular navigation apps that send a telecommunications signal to a satellite that bounces back to the cell phone to coordinate and pinpoint location versus destination, so too is the feedback transmitted at the end of a conversation. The listener provides a summary of the speaker's main points for affirmation or modification by the speaker to pinpoint the listener's understanding of the message. Depending upon the input of the speaker concerning the summary, adjustments may be needed for the fine tuning of the message.

When the listener provides the speaker with this sort of feedback during the conversation, the speaker feels heard, listened to, and understood. The mutual process is of benefit to the listener and speaker.

It allows the conversation to progress and both parties to arrive at the conversation destination together. A meeting of the minds can take place. The two become one by way of this reciprocal exchange. Furthermore, recapitulation also helps others in the room to understand the message if there is more than one person listening.

As we have seen in this discussion, providing feedback throughout the conversation creates a continuous loop which builds connections between the speaker and listener, listener and speaker. If you have provided the speaker with phrases such as "I see" during the conversation, if you have asked questions during the conversation, and if you have provided the speaker with a summary at the end of the conversation, you have established your credentials as an artful listener. The following model conversation illustrates how the listener utilizes these feedback strategies to create an artful conversation with the speaker.

MODEL CONVERSATION (Corporate Setting)
This conversation takes place in the office of William Brooks. He is Chief Executive Officer (CEO) for Dream Resorts in Orlando, Florida. Reginald Salisbury is the copywriter for the company's quarterly newsletter which is sent to the condominium owners at the company's six resorts in Nevada, Colorado and Florida. Fran Burke, one of William's administrative assistants, has called Reginald and asked him to report to William's office. Reginald has worked for William for about a year now; Reginald guesses that this conversation will be about the subject matter to be included in the next issue of the newsletter.

William is sitting behind his large desk, and Reginald takes a seat in front of the desk slightly to William's right and readies his pen and pad. (Since this is a formal business conversation, Reginald does not need to ask William's permission to take notes.) Having the pen and pad is crucial in conveying to William that Reginald is ready to listen. Using the pen and pad will be critical in helping Reginald retain the information that William is about to transmit. Reginald notices that the door has been left open, and so Reginald expects that there may be one or more interruptions during this conversation.

CEO (William): "Reginald, how are you this morning?"

COPYWRITER (Reginald): "Fine, sir."

EXPLANATION: Reginald knows that William has a no-nonsense management style and so waits patiently for him to begin.

CEO (William): "Good. Reginald, we are making some changes at our resort in Steamboat Springs, Colorado, and we need to let the condominium owners know about the changes in the next newsletter."

COPYWRITER (Reginald): "Yes, sir, go ahead."

EXPLANATION: Reginald is alerted to the subject of the conversation by William's repeated use of the word "changes." He writes the word "changes" in his notes and is already thinking about the timing of the changes. Reginald knows that for any change in resort operations he will need to include some sort of schedule in the article. Reginald may even write the word "schedule" next to the word "changes" at this early point in the conversation, especially as William pauses before his next point. This is a good example of how the listener can leverage the speech/understanding differential which is discussed earlier in this book.

CEO (William): "OK. After the ski season is over, the pool will be closed for resurfacing and painting. It will take about a month. The front desk will be open from 9 a.m. to

9 p.m. during the week but 24 hours a day on Saturday and Sunday for check-ins and check-outs. The shuttle bus service from the resort to the town of Steamboat Springs will be changed to Saturday and Sunday only. Have you got that?"

COPYWRITER (Reginald): "Yes, sir. Should I check with the front desk manager at the resort to verify the exact dates for the changes?"

EXPLANATION: Notice that Reginald does not interrupt William to ask him about the schedule for the changes. Instead, after William has finished speaking, Reginald answers, "Yes, sir" which informs William that Reginald is intelligently following along. Reginald then asks William if it is okay to contact the front desk manager about the schedule. He also makes sure to use the word "changes." This is an example of a listener repeating a word ("changes") used by the speaker to convey an understanding of the speaker's words.

CEO (William): "That's all right with me. On the sales side, the sales office will be closed on-site until the summer season. Owners may contact the salesperson through the front desk during regular front desk hours. By the way, we are letting Myers and Schaffer go. Only Newman will still be there after Friday."

COPYWRITER (Reginald): "I understand."

EXPLANATION: Reginald knows that only the information about the on-site sales office being closed will appear in the newsletter. He replies, "I understand" because he does not want to imply that he is agreeing with the layoffs that William has described. Saying "that sounds good" would not only be evaluative but would also imply that Reginald is glad that Myers and Schaffer are losing their jobs.

After Reginald says, "I understand," William is silent for a few seconds. Reginald maintains eye contact but does not speak. He understands that pauses and lulls are normal in these types of conversations. Reginald knows that silence is an effective listening tool in this situation; he patiently waits for William to speak again.

CEO (William): "Well, we better tell the owners in the newsletter about the special assessment coming next year. Let them know now before the annual meeting of the Steamboat Springs condominium owners. We have determined that the prior management company didn't fix the roof on any type of schedule, so we have to have a special assessment this year to fix it. The work will be finished next year, I think. Get with Phil Santos on the exact timing and the dollars."

COPYWRITER (Reginald): "OK. I will touch base with Mr. Santos about the schedule for the roof repair and the costs for the special assessment."

EXPLANATION: Notice the extent, richness, and amount of information received. Reginald's patience has paid off handsomely. Reginald has received William's message, restated and identified the key points, and provided William with good feedback. The quality of Reginald's feedback shows William that Reginald has understood William's message.

It is at this point that William's office phone rings. He pushes the button on the phone to activate the speaker. Fran Burke's voice is heard over the speaker.

ADMINISTRATIVE ASSISTANT (Fran): "Mr. Brooks, this is Fran. Your flight to Denver today is on time."

CEO (William, to Fran): "OK."

EXPLANATION: Phone calls are common interruptions in the workplace environment. Reginald waits silently for the call to be concluded.

CEO (William): "Where were we, Reginald?"

COPYWRITER (Reginald): "You told me to check with Mr. Santos about the schedule and costs for the special assessment at the Steamboat Springs resort."

EXPLANATION: Reginald can tell William the very last thing they discussed because 1) he just repeated the words to William a few seconds ago, and 2) he has captured the last words of the conversation in his notes.

CEO (William): "Yes. Did I tell you why we are doing it?"

COPYWRITER (Reginald): "Yes, sir. The prior management company didn't fix the roof on a regular schedule."

EXPLANATION: Reginald has captured the prior part of the conversation about the reason for the special assessment in his notes; therefore, it is easy for him to recall this information and paraphrase the information back to William. At this point, the Vice President of Sales, Don O'Brien, appears at the door of William's office.

VP of SALES (Don): "William, we are going to the Broadway Deli for lunch. Would you like to join us?"

CEO (William, to Don): "Yes. I think that we are done here. Just so you know, we are going to put the sales office closing at Steamboat Springs in the newsletter."

EXPLANATION: Another common interruption in the workplace is an executive walking into a meeting unannounced. Reginald was already prepared for such an interruption because he made a mental note at the beginning of the meeting that the door to the office was open. Reginald continues to listen.

VP of SALES (Don, to William): "William, what are you talking about? I've got 10 prospective buyers coming next week to the Steamboat office. We need a full sales force there at least until April 15."

CEO (William, to Don): "When did you set that up?"

VP of SALES (Don): "The final prospect confirmed over the weekend. I sent you an email this morning about it. Myers and Schaffer worked hard to get the appointments arranged."

EXPLANATION: This new information obviously contradicts the earlier statement by William that Myers and Schaffer were to be let go. Reginald realizes this and continues to listen artfully. William hesitates for a moment and then picks up the phone and calls Fran. He activates the speaker.

ADMINISTRATIVE ASSISTANT (Fran): "Yes, Mr. Brooks."

CEO (William, to Fran): "Did you get an email from O'Brien this morning about tours at Steamboat Springs?"

ADMINISTRATIVE ASSISTANT (Fran): "Yes, a hard copy is in the inbox on your desk."

EXPLANATION: William confirms with Fran that she did get the email from O'Brien. William then addresses Reginald.

CEO (William, to Reginald): "Reginald, hold up on the sales office closing. I will let you know what to write later. That's all for now."

COPYWRITER (Reginald, to William): "Yes, sir. To recap, in the article for the newsletter about the Steamboat resort, I will include the pool being closed, the front desk hours being changed, the shuttle schedule being revised, and the special assessment being planned for next year. Is that it so far?"

CEO (William, to Reginald): "Yes. So far."

COPYWRITER (Reginald, to William): "OK, sir."

CEO (William, to Don): "Don, let's talk more about this over lunch."

VP of SALES (Don, to William): "OK. Let's go."

EXPLANATION: This final verbal interaction illustrates the fluid nature of conversations within a dynamic work environment. Reginald keeps the note about the sales office closing but puts a question mark beside the note to signify the decision has not been made at the time of this conversation. The note may be important later if William brings up the issue again in a later meeting. Notice how Reginald makes an effective recap of the meeting which William tentatively confirms with the words "so far."

This conversation illustrates many of the feedback techniques that we have discussed in this section. There are many twists and turns in business conversations, and you as the artful listener have to be laser focused on the speaker's words as well as the way the words are expressed. Simply put, your job depends upon it.

Part III:

AFTER THE CONVERSATION

Tip 17:

Let the Speaker Contribute

Oftentimes, the most crucial question that you ask during the conversation may be the following: "Before we finish up, is there anything else that you would like to add to our conversation today?" This question is so important because it accomplishes two very important objectives that every artful listener has.

First, the speaker usually welcomes this invitation to speak his or her mind. As we have learned earlier in this book, the speaker is thirsting to be heard. Many times, the speaker himself or herself may not know exactly what is on his or her mind at any given second during the conversation. Therefore, this question may elicit a comment from the speaker that might surprise both the speaker and the listener. Second, the question signals a level of openness on the part of the listener that the speaker intuitively interprets as a sign of trust and receptivity.

Dr. Peter R. Malik, my trusted colleague and a contributor to this book, describes his experience concerning this issue in the following manner:

One of my class assignments in Freshman Composition was cast this way: "Take a survey of 20 students about a campus issue that you feel should be changed." This topic was taken to heart by many of my students who wanted to voice their own opinions about the topic as well as listen to the thoughts of their fellow students. The survey included this question: "Before we finish up, is there anything else that you would like to add to our conversation today?"

It was remarkable how well the question worked in bringing out ancillary issues concerning the topic as well as comments that were totally unrelated yet very instructive.

Here are some of the types of unusual responses that were prompted by the question:

Issue: Lack of Commuter Parking

Type of response to question about anything to add:

Too many spots are reserved for faculty members.

Issue: Dorm Conditions

Type of response to question about anything to add:

The dorm should be torn down, and a new one should be built.

Issue: Dorm Visitation Policy

Type of response to question about anything to add:

The freshmen should have the same visitation policy as all other students.

These types of comments indicate that 1) the speaker is letting the listener know what the root issue is, and 2) the speaker has enough trust in the listener to disclose to the listener what the speaker believes to be the unvarnished truth about the issue.

As I told my students, if you are not surprised by at least one response per 20 students interviewed, then your survey may either be unduly biased in some way in favor of your point of view, or the speakers do not have a sufficient level of trust in you as a listener to share what they are really feeling.

When you ask the speaker this question, prepare yourself to be surprised but, of course, do not immediately confront the speaker with your point of view. You are not there to win the argument but to exchange thoughts and ideas honestly in a spirit of kindness and cooperation. You are here to l-i-s-t-e-n.

Tip 18:
Thank the Speaker

Believe it or not, perhaps the most important part of spoken and written business communication is not the logic of your argument but the tone of it. Thus, the artful listener focuses intently on the tone created by the speaker's words. The words are only the tip of the iceberg. The artful listener seeks to listen to the full message—above and below, visible and invisible, audible and inaudible—to capture the iceberg of significance and meaning underneath the speaker's words.

In her book *Technical Writing*, Diana Reep defines tone as "the feelings conveyed by a message." According to Reep, "business correspondence should have a tone that sounds natural and conveys cooperation, mutual respect, sincerity, and courtesy."

Put simply, the tone to be conveyed in all spoken and written communication should be one of kindness and cooperation. Furthermore, the expression of appreciation is one of the most important ways of communicating kindness and cooperation to a listener or a reader.

Beginners in business communication are often motivated by a desire to talk a listener or a reader into accepting a decision. In response to a request by a customer for his or her down payment to be refunded in cash, the inexperienced or inadequately trained customer service representative may say something like this: "No cash refunds are allowed on purchases of less than $1,000." This type of response not only makes the situation worse but also may have an alienating effect on the customer. A more experienced and/or better trained business communicator would employ an artful listening approach to the encounter. Two rules of artful listening are applicable in this situation:

**Rule No. 1: People Do Not Care How Much We Know
Until They Know How Much We Care**

Applying this principle to the customer service scenario above requires a creative, artistic approach. What is at the top of the customer's mind? It is not the company policy but his or her needs, feelings, and emotions. In a nutshell, the customer wants to know that the representative cares. Such caring will be most perceived by the customer through both the representative's words and tone of voice. The customer will be keying in on this tone because the interaction is far more emotional than transactional, far more about dignity than dollars. The effective representative knows this and endeavors to convey (in Reep's words) "cooperation, mutual respect, sincerity, and courtesy" to the customer through a positive tone.

Rule No. 2: Seek First to Understand, Then to Be Understood

In his book entitled *The 7 Habits of Highly Effective People*, Stephen Covey discusses the fifth habit of highly effective people which is: "Seek first to understand, then to be understood." Covey's concept of "empathetic listening" involves listening with the goal of understanding the speaker's point of view as well as his or her feelings about the situation.

This is what the customer service representative who listens artfully accomplishes in conversations with customers. The representative mentally switches roles with the customer in an effort to see the issues from the customer's point of view. By combining the willingness to care with the ability to empathize, an effective customer service representative puts the "art" in his or her artful listening by expressing the same thought as noted above ("No cash refunds are allowed on purchases of less than $1,000") in words such as these: "Cash refunds are only allowed on purchases of $1,000 or more."

This is the heart or "art" of the matter. In the marketplace, and especially in the field of customer service, the word "no" should be used sparingly, if at all. It is a communication killer because "no" does many bad things: it disrupts further debate and dialogue; offends the listener's sensibilities; sends a message to the listener that the speaker is implacable; alters the environment of kindness and cooperation that has been so painstakingly created; and violates the trust between the speaker and listener. The damage is often irreversible.

With artful listening comes artful speaking, and one of the most artful ways to speak is to limit or eliminate the number of times that you say "no" in any given day. Try it. Here are some substitute words and phrases that flip the script from confrontation and rudeness to kindness and cooperation: "pass," "decline," "want to go in a different direction," and "are unable to move forward."

To conclude, you never lose money or face when you express your appreciation to a speaker. Even though the outcome of the conversation may not be as you might have wished, there is still no excuse for rudeness because it only makes the situation worse. You may feel good about your rudeness for a few seconds, but it may cost you a job opportunity or promotion and, more importantly, it *will* cost you your self-respect which is one of your most precious possessions. It can also extinguish the opportunity to build a meaningful relationship with the speaker far beyond the immediate transaction at hand.

In his book entitled *The Majesty of Calmness*, William George Jordan notes that "calmness is the rarest quality in human life. It is the poise of a great nature, in harmony with itself and its ideals." Therefore, always keep in mind the critical importance of calmness in your daily dealings with coworkers and superiors in the workplace. Everyone else may be losing his or her temper, but you must remain the model of temperance, the soul of kindness and cooperation.

Let your self-control be part of your reputation around the office. You will become the person that other employees seek out to float solutions and to create consensus. Expressing appreciation after every conversation helps to make you that person. By always giving thanks to the speaker, you are earning the sacred title of peacemaker.

Tip 19:
Wait for the Speaker to Signal the Departure

As noted earlier in this book, reading body language and exhibiting correct body language are two of the subtle ways of communicating effectively. In this case, you want to avoid giving the impression of trying to make a quick end of the interview. Instead, you desire to demonstrate the correct amount of respect to the speaker for his or her time and attention. Standing up abruptly and saying "bye bye" does not send the right message to the speaker. Artful listening is leading by listening. To lead by listening is exemplified when the artful listener is swift to listen and slow to speak or first to listen and last to speak. This is also true for the listener's body language.

In addition, such a stance puts the speaker first at the end of the conversational experience just as he or she should be at the beginning of the conversation and during the conversation itself. As we have learned, artful listening prioritizes receptivity over expressiveness and allows the listener to focus more on what the speaker wants to share than what the listener may be planning to share.

So wait patiently for the speaker to stand up before you begin to rise. Arise leisurely as if you had all the time in the world. Stand up as if you were in the company of a good friend, and you and your friend have just finished a fruitful conversation in which the friend spoke passionately, and you listened artfully.

Tip 20:
End the Physical Interaction
with the Speaker

As mentioned in the discussion concerning greeting the speaker in Tip 7: Introduce Yourself, the world is adjusting to a different reality in which greetings and farewells will involve little or no touching.

You may recall that my suggestions for greeting the speaker in that section included bowing slightly, nodding the head, and touching the heart.

For farewells, I prefer making a short, friendly wave along with saying a few sincere words such as the following: "It was great to see you. Goodbye."

However, you may employ one or more of the gestures that I have discussed previously along with words of your own choosing to create a farewell protocol that is unique to your personal style.

Remember that the simplest of gestures and words together can be the most powerful way to end a conversation.

Tip 21:
Write a Summary

There are many note-taking systems easily accessible on the Internet. The most straightforward is the Cornell system which was developed in the 1950s. Claire Brown, in an article entitled "What's the Best, Most Effective Way to Take Notes?" (available at theconversation. com/whats-the-best-most-effective-way-to-take-notes-41961), discusses this classic system in a cogent way.

I have modified the Cornell system based on my experience of taking notes and teaching the art of note-taking over the years. The principles follow:

1. A good listener is coming to the conversation with an outline already in mind. It is as follows: the speaker will have a theme (subject and attitude) to communicate to the listener during the conversation. In a conversation of 10 to 15 minutes, the speaker will make from two to four main points to support his or her theme. It is up to the listener to capture the theme and the points of support in the notes. Put another way, the listener should write down a note to every question and extrapolate a theme from the answers if the theme is not explicitly identified as such by the speaker.

2. It is absolutely critical to compose your summary of the conversation as soon as possible after the conversation.

3. I recommend the use of a Conversation Worksheet. As you begin the practice of note-taking and summarizing, the Conversation Worksheet can be simply a blank page. You may also set your worksheet up following the format shown in the first model conversation that appears later in this section.

4. On the Conversation Worksheet, always note the date, the name(s) of the participants in the conversation, and the location of the conversation at the top of the page.

5. Place the questions on the left hand side of the page, the answers on the right hand side of the page, and the summary at the bottom of the page.

6. Write the notes in phrases or short sentences and the summary in sentences.

7. Your summary should include the theme and the main points of the speaker in no more than eight sentences.

8. Once you are comfortable with this note-taking system, follow the principles each and every time that you take notes. It may seem time consuming at first. However, with practice, you will pick up speed, form a very important habit, and become an artful listener of every significant conversation that you will have in the future.

Dr. Malik describes his listening and note-taking experience in the following model conversation.

MODEL CONVERSATION (Academic Setting)

As a college teacher, I frequently queried my promising freshman composition students on whether they might consider changing their major to English. Here is a sample text of a possible conversation between myself and one of my composition students who stopped by my office to discuss this issue. A sample Conversation Worksheet about this talk follows the conversation text.

PROFESSOR (Dr. Malik): Good morning, Susan, and welcome. How can I help you?

STUDENT (Susan): I would like to talk to you about changing my major like you mentioned in class yesterday.

PROFESSOR (Dr. Malik): Sounds good. Can I ask you what your major is at this particular moment?

STUDENT (Susan): Yes, I am in biology right now.

PROFESSOR (Dr. Malik): I see. How did you come to pick biology as a major?

STUDENT (Susan): My dad was a biology major when he went here.

PROFESSOR (Dr. Malik): That happens a lot at this school. I already know that you are a good writer and speaker based on your class work. What do you like about English?

STUDENT (Susan): I love to read, and I used to write poetry when I was in high school. I also read stories to my niece. She loves it when I read books with her.

PROFESSOR (Dr. Malik): That's fine. Do you have a thought on what your future plans might be?

STUDENT (Susan): I might like to go into teaching.

PROFESSOR (Dr. Malik): Great. I can tell you that it is an extremely rewarding field. With a degree in English, you can teach at the high school level. Later, you could obtain a master's degree and then teach junior college courses. You can also attend law school. I think that you would make a great teacher or lawyer someday. How does that sound?

STUDENT (Susan): Good. I would like to try it.

PROFESSOR (Dr. Malik): OK. Since you are a freshman, you can switch to English and still graduate on time. So the next step is for you to meet with the department chairperson. I will check with her today and let you know a good time for you to meet with her.

STUDENT (Susan): OK.

PROFESSOR (Dr. Malik): OK, Susan, thanks for stopping by.

CONVERSATION WORKSHEET

DATE: March 17, 2016

PARTICIPANTS: Dr. Peter Malik and Susan Downs

MEETING PLACE: Lowell 212 (Dr. Peter Malik's Office)

QUESTIONS/SUGGESTIONS:	RESPONSES
What is major now?	Biology
Why did you pick it?	Dad majored in biology here
Why do you want to change to English?	Likes writing poetry and reading to her niece
What would you like to do as a career?	Might go into teaching
English is great for teachers and lawyers.	Understands
She will still graduate on time.	Understands
Should I set up a meeting with chairperson?	Yes

SUMMARY:

On March 17, 2016, I met with Susan Downs in Lowell 212. Susan is a biology major because her father did so when he was a student here. She likes writing poetry and reading stories to her niece. I let her know what English majors can do with the degree such as becoming teachers or lawyers. I also informed her that she can switch to English and still graduate on time. Susan agreed to meet with the department chairperson about changing her major to English.

Notice that the summary captures the answers to the questions posed during the conversation. The theme is also clearly stated: "Susan agreed to meet with the department chairperson about changing her major to English." Keep in mind that many conversations such as this one will have a theme that involves a course of action to be taken after the conversation has been concluded.

Let's take a look at a conversation in a sales setting at an automobile dealership. The sales representative is an artful listener who is attempting to identify her customers' needs about purchasing a vehicle. This type of representative seeks to build relationships, respect, and rapport with the prospective purchaser by listening carefully to the customers' needs and desires. The representative here asks questions to clarify her understanding of the customers' needs and also repeats and/or rephrases the customers' words so that the customers feel heard and understood. The sales representative works hard to establish a supportive environment in which a sale may occur naturally.

MODEL CONVERSATION (Sales Setting: Automobile Dealership)

Sue Johnson, the sales representative for an automobile dealership, talks with Fred and Dorothy Jones about their needs for a car.

> SALES REPRESENTATIVE (Sue): "Hi, I'm Sue Johnson. Glad to meet you."
>
> CUSTOMER (Fred): "I am Fred Jones, and this is my wife Dorothy."
>
> EXPLANATION: Sue greets Fred and Dorothy cordially. She writes Fred's and Dorothy's names on the worksheet. Sue

then uses their first names throughout the conversation.

SALES REPRESENTATIVE (Sue, to Fred and Dorothy): "Fred and Dorothy, what brings you in today?"

CUSTOMER (Fred): "We were thinking about getting a new car. Our old one is starting to break down too much."

EXPLANATION: Sue uses this question as a way to start the conversation in a friendly, non-confrontational manner.

SALES REPRESENTATIVE (Sue, to Fred): "So the car that you currently have is breaking down too much. Fred, would you be interested in a new car or a used used car today?"

CUSTOMER (Fred): "Probably a used car. It's for my wife to use around town mostly."

EXPLANATION: First, Sue restates and rephrases what she heard: "So the car you currently have is breaking down too much." Sue then asks Fred a question to determine his need for either a new or used car. His answer gives Sue the opportunity to bring Dorothy into the conversation.

SALES REPRESENTATIVE (Sue, to Dorothy): "Dorothy, may I ask you what you are driving at the moment?"

CUSTOMER (Dorothy): "A 2014 Honda CRV."

EXPLANATION: Sue's question continues the process of determining Fred's and Dorothy's needs for their next car.

SALES REPRESENTATIVE (Sue, to Dorothy): "A Honda CRV. Dorothy, Fred said that you will use the car around town. Tell me a little more about that."

CUSTOMER (Dorothy): "Well, I take my grandchildren to the park in it. I also go to art classes, and so I have a lot of paints and boards that I have to bring to class."

EXPLANATION: Sue repeats the term "CRV" to let Dorothy know that Sue is following Dorothy's thought process.

Next, Sue invites Dorothy to share her additional thoughts on how she will use the car.

SALES REPRESENTATIVE (Sue, to Dorothy): "Dorothy, you sound busy—taking the grandchildren to parks and going to art classes. What features would you like your next car to have?"

CUSTOMER (Dorothy): "Well, I would like to have another SUV because of all of my art materials. Plus we live on a street that floods sometimes when we get a hard rain."

EXPLANATION: Sue first rephrases the uses that Dorothy mentioned in her previous answer. Sue's question here is designed to connect these uses with the features that Dorothy desires in her next vehicle. Dorothy's answer indicates that she would like to have another SUV.

SALES REPRESENTATIVE (Sue, to Dorothy): "Thanks, Dorothy. I've noted your SUV choice because of your art interests and flood concerns."

SALES REPRESENTATIVE (Sue, to Fred): "Fred, what features would you like to see in the SUV?"

CUSTOMER (Fred): "It should be really safe with good sight lines. The one we have now has a bad blind spot. Plus it shouldn't drive like a truck."

EXPLANATION: Note how Sue artfully notes Dorothy's answer to show that she (Sue) has listened carefully to Dorothy's needs. Sue thanks Dorothy and then segues from Dorothy's answer to a question for Fred about his preferences in the SUV. Fred's answer reveals the features that he desires as well as the qualities in the SUV that he wants to avoid.

SALES REPRESENTATIVE (Sue, to Fred): "That's great, Fred. Thanks for letting me know. Do you have a price range in

> mind for the car at the moment?"
>
> CUSTOMER (Fred): "We are thinking about $15,000 to $17,000 if we trade in the Honda."
>
> EXPLANATION: Sue needs to find out the price range before showing Fred and Dorothy some possible vehicles for purchase so that she will not show them any cars too far below or above their price range.
>
> SALES REPRESENTATIVE (Sue, to Fred and Dorothy): "Sounds fair. Well, Fred and Dorothy, I have several cars in our inventory that I believe will fit your needs. Do you have any preference with regard to color?"
>
> CUSTOMER (Fred): "Yes. Royal blue. We love that color."
>
> EXPLANATION: This question and the answer complete the process. By using artful listening techniques, Sue has effectively listened from the customers' vantage point. Now she has enough information to identify which cars that she will show to Fred and Dorothy.

After the conversation, Sue notes the date, the names of the participants, and the location of the conversation on the Conversation Worksheet. Sue writes the questions down on the left side of the worksheet and records Fred's and Dorothy's answers on the right side of the worksheet. She completes a summary of the conversation on the blank lines at the bottom of the worksheet.

A reasonable summary of this conversation might look like this:

I met with Fred and Dorothy Jones on April 11, 2018 at the dealership. Fred and Dorothy are looking to purchase a car for Dorothy to drive around town with her grandchildren and to go to her art classes. She currently drives a 2014 Honda CRV. Dorothy would like her next car to have plenty of room for her art supplies and to sit higher off the ground like the SUV that she and Fred currently own because their street floods. Her husband Fred says that the car should be safe with no bad blind spots. Their price range is $15,000 to $17,000 after they trade in their current vehicle.

This brings us to an artful conversation that routinely takes place in the field of real estate sales when a prospective purchaser has his or her first meeting with a realtor.

MODEL CONVERSATION (Sales Setting: Real Estate)

Carla Jackson graduated from the University of Nevada, Las Vegas five years ago with a degree in accounting. She currently works as an accountant for a major hotel on the west side of Las Vegas. Carla has been renting a two-bedroom house for $1,200 a month. She is interested in purchasing a condo in the same neighborhood where she is renting. Her friend Patrice Jordan knows a realtor in town named Jason Collier. Carla is meeting with Jason for the first time in Jason's office.

> REALTOR (Jason): "Hi, I'm Jason Collier. You must be Carla. Good to meet you."
>
> CUSTOMER (Carla): "Yes, I am Carla Jackson. It's good to meet you as well."
>
> EXPLANATION: Jason knows Carla's name already through Patrice.
>
> REALTOR (Jason): "Please have a seat at my conference table. Might I offer you a bottle of spring water?"
>
> CUSTOMER (Carla): "No, thank you. I am good right now."
>
> EXPLANATION: The question is a worthwhile effort to make the speaker comfortable; it sends a signal of patience and

willingness to listen.

REALTOR (Jason): "Carla, I understand from Patrice that you might be interested in buying a condo in town. Is that right?"

CUSTOMER (Carla): "That's right. I am renting a two-bedroom house right now for $1,200 a month near the Orleans Hotel, and I am tired of paying rent."

EXPLANATION: Jason's question is a good way to start the conversation on a friendly note.

REALTOR (Jason): "Well, I can certainly understand that you might be tired of paying rent every month. Carla, may I ask you if you have purchased property before?"

CUSTOMER (Carla): "No, I have not, and I am not sure how the whole process works."

EXPLANATION: Jason needs to determine if Carla is a first-time home buyer. First-time buyers typically need more information about the buying process itself than people who have purchased property in the past. First-time home buyers may also have access to funding opportunities unavailable to repeat buyers. Thus, after obtaining this information by listening carefully, Jason will be able to deliver a more personalized and delightful customer service experience.

REALTOR (Jason): "OK, I will be glad to walk you through the entire process. There's nothing in the world like owning your own place. We should start with the budget that you have in mind. With regard to the monthly payment for the condo, are you comfortable with higher or a lower monthly payment than what you are paying now?"

CUSTOMER (Carla): "I would like to pay the same amount that I am paying."

EXPLANATION: Carla previously disclosed to Jason the amount that she is currently paying for rent. Now Jason is starting to determine the general price range that Carla can afford.

REALTOR (Jason): "OK. When you purchase a property, you have to put up a certain percentage of the purchase price as a down payment. The minimum is usually five percent. That could be from $5,000 to $10,000 depending on the purchase price of the condo. What amount do you think might be affordable to you for a down payment at this particular time?"

CUSTOMER (Carla): "Well, I could probably put up as much as $10,000 if I had to."

EXPLANATION: Jason is informing Carla about the need for a down payment. She informs him of the maximum amount of money that she has available for a down payment.

REALTOR (Jason): "Excellent. I also would like to let you know that every condominium complex requires a monthly fee for maintaining the property. It's called an HOA fee, which stands for Homeowners Association fee. The fee varies from property to property. I will let you know the HOA for each property that we visit."

CUSTOMER (Carla): "I understand."

EXPLANATION: Jason discloses the information about the HOA fee so that Carla understands the special expenses involved in owning a condominium.

REALTOR (Jason): "Now, Carla, I have a friend named Nancy Mason who helps many first-time buyers with the financing of their property. If you want, I can have Nancy reach out to you by text or email, and you can meet with her at your convenience. Once your financing is in place, we will be ready to visit some properties for sale. Would that be okay?"

CUSTOMER (Carla): "Yes, that is all right with me."

EXPLANATION: The meeting with Nancy Mason is important because once the financial institution verifies Carla's buying power, Jason will only show Carla the properties that are in this price range.

REALTOR (Jason): "OK. Now we are coming to the fun part. Do you want to stay in the same area where you live now?"

CUSTOMER (Carla): "I think so. I want to be near work. I am an accountant at the Orleans."

EXPLANATION: After budget, the next part of any conversation about real estate has to be about location. Jason needs to know at this point in the conversation if Carla wants to be in the same location or move to some other part of town.

REALTOR (Jason): "I understand. That's great to hear. Are you interested in a one- or two-bedroom unit?"

CUSTOMER (Carla): "Hopefully a two-bedroom unit, so my dog has his own room."

EXPLANATION: After location, Jason needs to know Carla's thinking about the size of the unit. She has also volunteered that she owns a dog. Jason knows that some condominium properties allow pets, and some do not. He will be sure to remember to show Carla only those properties for sale which are pet friendly.

REALTOR (Jason): "Carla, can I ask you what features that you must have in your condo?"

CUSTOMER (Carla): "I definitely want it to be dog friendly. Also, I want a condo with a pool and a workout room or gym. I drive to the gym now, and I want to have one right where I live."

EXPLANATION: Jason's question about "must have" features is a polite way of asking Carla about her basic requirements for the condo. Jason will ensure that every property that he shows to Carla offers these features.

REALTOR (Jason): "I am glad to know that. Are there any other features that you might like?"

CUSTOMER (Carla): "I would love a little fireplace and maybe a balcony."

EXPLANATION: Jason is determining the features that Carla "might like" to have in her new condo. This means such features are desirable but are not required by her.

REALTOR (Jason): "OK, I see: one that is dog friendly with a pool and gym for sure and perhaps a fireplace and balcony. Carla, there are some beautiful condos in the area around the Orleans Hotel. I will be happy to set up some showings for you. In the meantime, you can have a conversation with Nancy and determine a price range that is affordable for you. I am sure that Nancy will do her best to meet your needs. Does that sound like a good plan?"

CUSTOMER (Carla): "Yes, that sounds fine."

EXPLANATION: Jason verifies Carla's list of "must have" and "might like" features and reiterates the future course of action that he will take in Carla's home-buying journey. He also assures Carla that Nancy will be her friend and ally in the process.

REALTOR (Jason): "Very good. I can't wait to show you what's available."

CUSTOMER (Carla): "Thank you. I am ready to go for it."

> EXPLANATION: Jason concludes the conversation by communicating his excitement to Carla about the next step in the process.

As in previous examples, Jason notes the date, names of participants, and location of the conversation at the top of the Conversation Worksheet. He then writes the questions down on the left side of the worksheet and records Carla's answers on the right side of the worksheet. He completes a summary of the conversation on the blank lines at the bottom of the worksheet.

The summary of this conversation might look like this:

On September 12, 2019, I met with Carla Jackson in the Collier Realty office on Decatur Boulevard in Las Vegas. Carla wants to purchase a two-bedroom condominium on the west side of Las Vegas near the Orleans Hotel where she works. Carla desires to have a monthly payment of around $1,200 a month, and she has up to $10,000 for a down payment. She is open to meeting with Nancy Mason about financing. Carla understands that there is an HOA fee for any condo that she might purchase. She wants to buy within a condominium complex which is dog friendly and has a pool and a gym. Her wish list includes a fireplace and a balcony. I will set up showings of available properties for Carla after she has met with Nancy.

The theme is stated in the second sentence of the summary, and the points of support appear in the succeeding sentences. In this case, the future course of action is disclosed in the last sentence of the summary.

Tip 22:
Send a Timely
Expression of Thanks

The artful listener's work is not done after the conversation has been concluded. It is imperative that you follow up the conversation with a communication either in a handwritten note or by email in which you thank the speaker for his or her time and make mention of the outcome of the conversation that was just finished. Here is a sample of a follow-up email of this type:

> Dear (Speaker's Full Name):
>
> Thank you very much for meeting with me today. I very much appreciated your time and thoughts. I learned a lot about (subject) during our conversation. I hope that we will be able to communicate with each other about this topic in the future.
>
> Thanks again for our conversation.
>
> (Listener's Full Name)

Please see page 130 for a discussion of a thank-you note sent from an applicant to the job interviewer after the interview has been completed. A model thank-you note also appears on that page.

The Artful Listener's Guide

to the Job Interview Process

by Dr. Peter R. Malik

I. Here is what to do before the interview.

I used to tell my graduating seniors to ask for graduation gifts such as a good leather portfolio (preferably one that zips all the way around) as well as personalized stationery and envelopes. These two items are valuable tools in your job quest. You will use the portfolio to store your business cards and copies of your cover letter, resume, and list of references that might be needed during the interview. The personalized stationery and envelopes will be utilized when you write a handwritten note to the interviewer after the interview.

So you have received a call from the prospective employer's representative, Mr. Fred Garcia, and your interview has been arranged for Tuesday, March 31 at 1 p.m. Your quest for employment begins now—and so too must your preparation.

The interview is set for Tuesday at 1 p.m. When do you go? You should plan to arrive about five to eight minutes before 1 p.m. on *Monday.*

A. Go to the interview location 24 hours in advance.

Yes, that is right: go to your interview 24 hours in advance. How come? Here are two good reasons to do so:

1. There is something called lunch rush hour in big cities.

   Your interview is set for 1 p.m. and Google Maps or GPS tells you that your journey should take 35 minutes. Is that on a Sunday or Monday? Is that at 6 a.m. or noon? Do not trust your future to an algorithm. Depart at 12:15 p.m. on Monday and see how long it really takes to reach your destination.

2. Construction happens at the most unfortunate times.

   Maybe those navigational apps take construction into consideration, but do not count on it. If you are supposed to take the Westheimer Road exit and the Westheimer Road exit is congested or closed due to road work, your anxiety level will go up, and your confidence level will go down. Your trip on Monday will help you to familiarize yourself with the route to the job interview as it exists in the real world.

B. Scout the location of the job interview.

Again, do not trust apps. It looks like one office building in the street view, but the location turns out to be an office park with 17 separate but identical buildings. You look at the address of the first one, and the sign says 13B, and you know that your interview is in 31C. Your anxiety goes up, and your confidence goes down. You tell yourself that you will ask at the guard shack, but the guard shack is empty, and there is a handwritten sign on the window that says, "Be back at 1." It is safe to say that the guard may not appear exactly at 1 p.m.

C. Enter the building and locate Mr. Garcia's office.

There will be a directory in the lobby, and you will use it to find Mr. Garcia's office. Proceed to that office. There will be a person in the reception area (let's call her Sally) who is Mr. Garcia's administrative assistant. This is a key person for you to meet. Introduce yourself this way: "Hi, I am (your name), I have a meeting with Mr. Garcia tomorrow at 1 p.m. I just wanted to make sure that I am in the right place." Sally will probably reply in this fashion: "I am Sally Cook, Mr. Garcia's assistant, and yes, this is his office."

D. Engage with Mr. Garcia's assistant.

Now that you have met Sally, it is time to gather your courage and interact with her as an artful listener. Say something like

113

this: "Sally, this looks like a great place to work. How do you like working here?" In reply, Sally will say one of three things: "It's okay," "Oh, you are going to love it," or "Well, I have been with Mr. Garcia for several years, and it really *is* good."

Let us analyze these responses using an artful listening approach:

1. "It's okay." Notice how what is not said reveals something about the environment of this particular workplace. The reply also means that Sally does not really want to engage in any further conversation.

2. "Oh, you are going to love it." Use your artful listening skills on this one. Art may reveal by what it conceals. Listen behind the words and hear what was not said. Is this sentence spoken with a hint of sarcasm? Even if you detect a sarcastic tone, that still gives you important information about the workplace environment at this office.

3. "Well, I have been with Mr. Garcia for several years, and it really *is* good." This is the hoped-for answer that indicates the environment and the position may be just right for you.

Regardless of her reply, I suggest that you say this: "Thank you. Would you have any other information about the company that's not on the website?" The answer will probably be "no." However, if you are lucky, Sally will say, "You know, the employee newsletter just came out. You may have a copy if you would like." She then hands you a copy. You say, "Thanks, Sally, I enjoyed meeting you, and I will see you tomorrow." You depart the office.

E.   Complete your mission.

However, you are still not finished with your reconnaissance mission. Find a convenience store and a post office near the building where Mr. Fred Garcia's office is located and note their locations. You will visit both of these places tomorrow on the day of the interview.

F.   Go home and study.

On the night before the interview, you want to learn as much as you can about the company. You particularly want to read the President's Message (usually available on the website) for hints about the growth prospects of the company. You want to go into the interview tomorrow knowing as much as you can about the company's culture, products, services, and/or marketing strategy along with its plans for the future. It is also important to review your social media accounts to ensure that you have not posted any messages or photos that portray you in a manner that would be unappealing to employers. As noted earlier in the book, it is recommended that you purchase a leather portfolio. Tonight, place your business cards and copies of your cover letter, resume, and list of references in the portfolio for possible use during the interview. Also, if you have personalized stationery, make sure to put the stationery with stamps in your car for use tomorrow after the interview.

Before we move on, it is helpful to note all of the benefits that you have received from preparing one day in advance. You have made all of your navigational mistakes, you have found the correct building, you have met Mr. Garcia's assistant, you have taken the temperature of what it is like to work there, and you may have received additional information about the company. You went home and read the information from cover to cover and researched the company thoroughly on its website. You should sleep soundly now.

G. Follow your normal routine during the morning of the interview.

Wake up at the usual time and follow your regular routine for preparing for a workday. One powerful strategy for men is to dress in your best suit. Wear a t-shirt with your suit and place a dry-cleaned shirt and a new tie in your car. Take a leisurely drive to the convenience store that you found yesterday nearest the building. Go in and buy your favorite non-alcoholic drink. Visit the restroom with your dry-cleaned shirt and new tie and don the shirt and tie in the restroom. Comb or brush your hair once more. By this time on a summer day, many other applicants may look wrinkled and uncomfortable when they arrive for the interview. In contrast, your clothing will look crisp and clean, and you will look cool and confident.

H. Arrive at the reception area five to eight minutes before 1 p.m.

If you get there too early, you might be perceived as a nuisance or as an overeager (read desperate) applicant. Show up in the five- to eight-minute window. Keep in mind that, in this time frame, you might see one or two other applicants sitting in the waiting area. This is due to the fact that Mr. Garcia may be running behind with his interviews. Do not worry about the other applicants. You are probably much more prepared than they are for the interview.

I. Engage with Sally.

Sally is at her desk, and you approach the desk and say, "Good afternoon, Sally, I took a look at the information that you gave me yesterday, and now I am even more excited about working here."

Sally will probably say, "Good. Have a seat. Mr. Garcia will be with you shortly."

Now this might happen when Sally goes back to Mr. Garcia's office to let him know that you have arrived. Behind the closed door of his office, Mr. Garcia may ask Sally this question: "How does he look?" Sally has been with Mr. Garcia for six years, and he knows that the new employee must interact with Sally well. So Sally's answer gives him a pretty good idea of the candidate's potential before Mr. Garcia ever meets you.

Usually, Sally's reply will be "OK." That means she does not want to influence Mr. Garcia's judgment one way or the other. However, in your case, she will say, "He (or she) came by yesterday to find our office." If Sally volunteers such information, Mr. Garcia will instantly recognize that you are a serious candidate. In this way, you have made a positive impression on Mr. Garcia before he meets you because of the preparation that you did yesterday.

J. Engage with Mr. Garcia.

As previously discussed in this book, you want to stride confidently into Mr. Garcia's office, make eye contact, and offer your preferred type of physical greeting such as bowing slightly, nodding the head, or touching the heart while you say, "Hello, I'm (your name)."

An interview is both relational and transactional. Therefore, as you enter the office, look around and notice what is on the wall or

117

the desk. You want to make a human connection with Mr. Garcia before you make a logical connection during the interview. See if there is something on the desk or the wall that you can mention quickly. If you see a Chicago Cubs poster or trinket, say, "Wasn't it great that the Cubs finally won the World Series?" That comment will endear you to any Cubs fan. If you were in a fraternity or sorority in college and you see any evidence of fraternity or sorority membership, you can say something like this: "Were you in a Greek letter organization? I'm a Sigma." Any connection that you make with the interviewer prior to the actual interview improves your chances of getting hired.

II. Here is what to do during the interview.

Once you and the interviewer are seated, you start a clock ticking in your head: 15 minutes. This is what the interviewer has in his or her head too. You should expect about 10 questions, and so each one of your answers should be about 90 seconds long. If you spend six minutes on the first question, you will not get the job. Your answers should be short and succinct. It is very important to keep that 15-minute clock in your head during the entire length of the interview. Your prior preparation and practice will be of great benefit in keeping with the time frame.

For many years, the No. 1 result on Google for the search term "Top 10 Interview Questions" was an article entitled "Prep for the Top 10 Interview Questions" by Carole Martin. It is probable that your competitors for the job found Martin's article online and used it for their preparation. Some of the answers that she suggests are quite good, but the answers that I put forth below are designed to present a strong, comprehensive argument that *you* are the ideal candidate for the position.

I will start with this question which is not on Martin's list.

"Tell me about yourself."

This is a softball question meant for you to hit out of the park. What the interviewer is looking for is an answer that is short and sweet. More importantly, he or she wants to know if you have prepared in advance for the interview or if you are just planning on winging it.

Here is my suggested answer:

"I grew up in (city, state).

I graduated from (college) in (year) with a degree in (name of degree). At (name of college), I was a member of (name of organization).

In my spare time, I like to (name of activity)."

This answer provides the interviewer with some basic information about you. It also demonstrates that you are a disciplined, prepared applicant. Remember that every interview question is designed at some level to see how well you listen. Again, the key is to be clear and succinct. Employ your artful listening techniques and never miss a chance to be quiet.

We will now proceed to Carole Martin's list of 10 questions, her suggested answers, and the answers that I have found over the years to be powerful and effective.

Carole Martin's Question No. 1:

"What are your weaknesses?"

Her suggested answer:

"I am always working on improving my communication skills to be a more effective presenter. I recently joined Toastmasters, which I find very helpful."

Her explanation:

This is the most dreaded question of all. Handle it by minimizing your weakness and emphasizing your strengths. Stay away from personal qualities and concentrate on professional traits.

My suggested answer:

"Sometimes I work all the way up to the last minute of a deadline because I can't let anything go unless it's perfect."

My explanation:

This is a trap question that is meant to throw you off balance. The interviewer is expecting a "deer in the headlights" look. This answer avoids the trap and presents the interviewer with two of your most admirable traits, the ability to meet deadlines and the talent to generate error-free work product.

Carole Martin's Question No. 2

"Why should we hire you?"

Her suggested answer:

"With five years' experience working in the financial industry and my proven record of saving the company money, I could make a big difference in your company. I'm confident I would be a great addition to your team."

Her explanation:

Summarize your experiences.

My suggested answer:

"My education and experience make me a perfect fit for the position. Plus I have the motivation to help the company meet its goals."

My explanation:

Remember that the interviewer may have been the one who reviewed your resume and called you in for an interview. This answer reinforces the interviewer's own positive judgment that your background is suited for the position. You have also introduced the word "goals" into the conversation which will be important later. Finally, the interviewer will notice and appreciate the succinctness of your answer.

Carole Martin's Question No. 3

"Why do you want to work here?"

Her suggested answer:

"I've selected key companies whose mission statements are in line with my values, where I know I could be excited about what the company does, and this company is very high on my list of desirable choices."

Her explanation:

The interviewer is listening for an answer that indicates you've given this some thought and are not sending out resumes just because there is an opening.

My suggested answer:

"You are a leader in your industry. I went to your company's website and I read President Edgar Solomon's statement that your goal is to expand to 12 locations next year. I want to be part of that growth."

My explanation:

This is a key answer in the interview. You are displaying your knowledge of the company in a compelling way. Plus you are echoing the word "goals" that you mentioned in an answer to a prior question. It is possible that the press release with this information that you read last night on the website was published yesterday when the interviewer was tied up in meetings. It is possible that he or she has not read it yet. This means for this one moment you know more about the company than he or she does.

This is when the fun starts. The interviewer may have been appearing to be mildly bored or otherwise disengaged so far in the interview. That was an act. After you offer the suggested answer, watch his or her body language change. Now he or she will start to assume a straighter, more professional posture. The interviewer is starting to think that you are the one.

Carole Martin's Question No. 4

"What are your goals?"

Her suggested answer:

"My immediate goal is to get a job in a growth-oriented company. My long-term goal will depend on where the company goes. I hope to eventually grow into a position of responsibility."

Her explanation:

Sometimes it's best to talk about short-term and intermediate goals rather than locking yourself into the distant future.

My suggested answer:

"My immediate goal is to get a job in a growth-oriented company such as yours. My long-term goal will depend on where the company goes and what future opportunities may be presented."

My explanation:

The artful listener will discern the thought behind this question. The interviewer is really asking not so subtly if you are going to be after his or her job from your first day of employment forward. There is no way that you will be hired if your goal is to replace the person who is making the decision to hire you. This is one of those no-win questions. Punt it.

Carole Martin's Question No. 5

"Why did you leave (or why are you leaving) your job?"

Her suggested answer:

"I managed to survive two rounds of corporate downsizing, but the third round was a 20 percent reduction in the workforce, which included me."

"After two years, I made the decision to look for a company that is team-focused, where I can add my experience."

Her explanation:

For the first answer: If you're unemployed, state your reason for leaving in a positive context. For the second answer: If you are employed, focus on what you want in your next job.

My suggested answer:

"I had gone as far as I could in that position. I wanted more opportunity to learn and grow."

My explanation:

This is another tough question if you have not prepared for it. My suggested answer reinforces your theme throughout the interview that you want to "grow." Almost any other answer sounds like an excuse.

Carole Martin's Question No. 6:

"When were you most satisfied in your job?"

Her suggested answer:

"I was very satisfied in my last job, because I worked directly with the customers and their problems; that is an important part of the job for me."

Her explanation:

The interviewer wants to know what motivates you. If you can relate an example of a job or project when you were excited, the interviewer will get an idea of your preferences.

My suggested answer:

"I was very satisfied in my last job because I worked directly with the customers and created solutions for them; that is an important part of the job for me. I like to help people."

My explanation:

The artful listener listens in a way that encourages others to speak, and he or she speaks in a manner that encourages others to listen artfully. The interviewer does not want to hear the word "problem"; he or she wants to hear the word "solution." In addition, the sentence "I like to help people" will appeal to every interviewer for every company in every business. You are showing in your answer that you are the candidate who can meet the universal need in the workplace for employees who can create solutions altruistically.

Carole Martin's Question No. 7

"What can you do for us that other candidates can't?"

Her suggested answer:

"I have a unique combination of strong technical skills, and the ability to build strong customer relationships. This allows me to use my knowledge and break down information to be more user-friendly."

Her explanation:

What makes you unique? This will take an assessment of your experiences, skills and traits. Summarize concisely.

My suggested answer:

"I don't know about all of the other candidates, but I can tell you one thing: I will never let you down."

My explanation:

Here you are just being honest. You simply have no idea about all of the other candidates' levels of education and work experiences. So you mention the trait that you possess that all employers need: loyalty. It is the secret sauce of the successful interview. It is a phrase that interviewers love to hear.

Carole Martin's Question No. 8

"What are three positive things your last boss would say about you?"

Her suggested answer:

"My boss has told me that I am the best designer he has ever had. He knows he can rely on me, and he likes my sense of humor."

Her explanation:

It's time to pull out your old performance appraisals and boss's quotes. This is a great way to brag about yourself through someone else's words.

My suggested answer:

"My last supervisor, (name of supervisor), would say that I am smart, talented, and I always find a way to get the job done."

My explanation:

This is a softball question for the artful listener. This question is actually a listening test. The interviewer wants to see if you focused on the most important word in the question which is "three." If you mention two positive things, you lose. If you mention four positive things, you lose. In both instances ("two" or "four"), you lose because you demonstrate with these answers that you did not listen. My suggested answer is short, succinct, and easy to remember. You are also projecting the three traits that all employers desire in their employees.

Carole Martin's Question No. 9

"What salary are you seeking?"

Her suggested answer:

One possible answer would be: "I am sure when the time comes, we can agree on a reasonable amount. In what range do you typically pay someone with my background?"

Her explanation:

It is to your advantage if the employer tells you the range first. Prepare by knowing the going rate in your area and your bottom line or walk-away point.

My suggested answer:

"I went to salary.com and I found out that the average starting salary for an entry-level accounting position in (city, state) is $55,000 per year. Is that in your range?"

My explanation:

You are probably not comfortable talking about the money, so this answer provides a solution to that reticence. You simply quote a credible third-party source that is easily accessible to the interviewer. The key to this answer is to say it and then be quiet. In reply, the interviewer will probably say this: "That's a little high, but it's somewhere in the range." You instantly know that the salary for the job is probably budgeted for 20 percent below the average range or about $44,000 per year.

Carole Martin's Question No. 10

"If you were an animal, which one would you want to be?"

Her suggested answer:

If you answer "a bunny," you will make a soft, passive impression. If you answer "a lion," you will be seen as aggressive.

Her explanation:

Interviewers use this type of psychological question to see if you can think quickly. What type of personality would it take to get the job done? What impression do you want to make?

My suggested answer:

"I would be an eagle because I like to soar."

My explanation:

This question is an example of the type of personal question(s) that you may be asked to see how well you can think on your feet. My suggested answer is reasonable and safe.

Here's another personal question that has gained more popularity in recent years: "Describe a major failure of yours and what you learned from it." This one is also relatively easy to overcome. My suggested answer is as follows: "You know, I lost my focus during my freshman year in college, and my grades were not where they should have been. I quickly motivated myself to get on the right track, and I wound up graduating with honors." This answer capitalizes on the fact that nearly everyone who ever attended college lost focus during freshman year, and that possibly includes the interviewer himself or herself. It is another trap question that is easily met and resolved.

You will probably get this last question: "Do you have any questions for me?" This one is a pro forma question signaling the end of the interview. You may answer it in two ways. The first is to say, "Not really, I am just ready to go to work." The second is to say, "Will I work directly for you?" If the answer is "yes," then you give the artful listener's response: "I am really glad to hear that." If the answer is no, write down the name of the person who will be your supervisor and say, "Well, I am certainly looking forward to meeting him (or her)."

The interviewer is probably not going to hire you on the spot. Instead, the interviewer will say something like this: "We have some more interviews to do, and we will be calling the top candidates back later this week. Is the number that I have for you still a good one?" After you have answered this question, the interview is now concluded.

As you begin to leave, consider using the same gesture that you used to greet the interviewer (bowing slightly, nodding the head, or touching the heart) while saying something like this: "It was great to meet you. Goodbye now." Exit the interview space, but do not forget to say goodbye to Sally if at all possible before you leave the building.

III. Here is what to do after the interview.

You have also previously identified the post office nearest to the building where the interview took place. Using the personalized stationery that you placed in your car last night, you now write a personal thank-you note to the interviewer while you are sitting in your car. Here is a model for that communication:

> Date
>
> Dear (Interviewer's Name):
>
> Thank you for conducting our interview today about the position of (name of position) that you have available with (name of company).
>
> I thoroughly enjoyed our conversation. After learning more about the position and the company, I believe that my education and experience truly make me an excellent candidate for the position. At this point, I am even more excited about coming to work for (name of company).
>
> Thank you for your consideration of my application. I look forward to hearing from you soon.
>
> Name

After you finish writing the note, put it in the envelope, address and seal the envelope, and place a stamp on the envelope. Proceed to the post office and drop the letter in the mail. Depending on the time of day of your interview, your thank-you letter should reach the interviewer within 24-48 hours of the interview.

What will all the other applicants do? They will probably write a short email to the interviewer within a day or two. It's a nice gesture but easy and not very personal. In contrast, your handwritten note will be read carefully by the interviewer. He or she will be impressed that you went the extra mile to express your appreciation and to communicate your interest about the position in a very timely and personal manner. This extra effort is what puts the "art" in artful listening.

22 Memorable Quotes about the Divine Art of Listening

The following quotes encapsulate what I believe about the art of listening in all of its wonderful complexity. These thoughts have been gleaned from literary, nonfiction, and sacred sources.

Attention is the rarest and purest form of generosity.
–Simone Weil

It takes two to speak the truth—one to speak and another to hear.
–Henry David Thoreau

Listen to silence. It has so much to say.
–Rumi

You cannot truly listen to anyone and do anything else
at the same time.
–M. Scott Peck

The most important thing in communication
is hearing what isn't said.
–Peter Drucker

You can be an artist who works with oil paints or marble, sure.
But there are artists who work with numbers, business models,
and customer conversations. Art is about intent
and communication, not substances.
–Seth Godin

Every person in this life has something to teach me—
and as soon as I accept that, I open myself to truly listening.
–Catherine Doucette

The first duty of love is to listen.
–Paul Tillich

You must let suffering speak, if you want to hear the truth.
–Cornel West

Whoever has ears ought to hear.
–Matthew 11:15

The universal door manifests itself
in the voice of the rolling tide.
Hearing and practicing it, we become a child,
born from the heart of a lotus,
fresh, pure, and happy,
capable of speaking and listening
in accord with the universal door.
–Lotus Sutra

People start to heal the moment they feel heard.
–Cheryl Richardson

Listening is a magnetic and strange thing, a creative force.
The friends who listen to us are the ones we move toward.
When we are listened to, it creates us, makes us unfold
and expand.
–Karl Menninger

If we can share our story with someone who responds
with empathy and understanding, shame can't survive.
–Brené Brown

It's not at all hard to understand a person;
it's only hard to listen without bias.
–Criss Jami

I tried to discover, in the rumor of forests and waves, words that
other men could not hear, and I pricked up my ears to listen
to the revelation of their harmony.
–Gustave Flaubert

Never miss a good chance to shut up.
–Will Rogers

Listening isn't just about being quiet.
It's about listening to—
What is Said,
What is Unsaid,
and
What is meant
With your Eyes, Ears and Heart.
–Drishti Bablani

Pheoby's hungry listening helped Janie to tell her story.
–Zora Neale Hurston

To listen means to know and to acknowledge another and to allow him to step into the realm of one's own "I."
–Pope Benedict XVI

There is music the moment you start listening.
–Marty Rubin

Our heart breathes through the ear.
–Francis de Sales

Bibliography of Publications by Dr. John G. Igwebuike

Igwebuike, John G. "Effective Listening: Discover Why Good
Listeners Get More Jobs!" *Career Connections*, 2011,
pp. 53-54, calameo.com/books/000639011be3ca5023f4e.

—. "The Key to Effective Listening." *The Toastmaster*, April 2002,
pp. 12-13.

—. "Legal and Policy Implications for Faculty Diversification in
Higher Education." *Negro Educational Review,* vol. 57, no. 3/4,
Fall 2006, pp. 189–201, 265.

—. "Lesson 7: Effective Listening: The Secret Sauce of Diversity
Consultants." *The Diversity Consultant Cookbook:
Preparing for the Challenge,* written and edited by
Eddie Moore, Jr., Art Munn, and
Marguerite W. Penick-Parks, Stylus, 2019.

—. Review of *How to Teach Students Who Don't Look Like You:
Culturally Relevant Teaching Strategies* by Bonnie M. Davis.
National Academic Advising Association, 2006.

—. Review of *The University in the Global Age* by Roger King.
National Academic Advising Association Journal,
vol. 33, no. 2, Spring 2013.

—. "When Two Advanced Degrees Are Not Enough." *Brothers of the
Academy: Up and Coming Black Scholars Earning Our
Way in Higher Education*, edited by Lee Jones,
Stylus, 2000, pp. 221-29.

Igwebuike, John G., and Kendall D. Isaac. "Employer Implications of
Conducting Background Checks in the Post-911 Environment."
American University Labor & Employment Law Forum,
vol. 4, no. 1, 2014, pp. 46-65.

Igwebuike, John G., and William E. Pinney. "A Decision-Theoretic Framework for Strategic Legal Decisions." *Journal of Behavioral Studies in Business*, vol. 1, no. 1, 2009, pp. 55-60.

Udemgba, Benedict, and John Igwebuike. "Stock Options Backdating Scandals: What Do Market Participants Think about the Investigations?" *Journal of Behavioral Studies in Business*, 2009.

Audio/Video Resources

Igwebuike, John G. "Broadcast in Education." *Blog Talk Radio*, 22 July 2013, www.blogtalkradio.com/ intersectionsradio/2013/07/22/guest-dr-john-igwebuike.

—. "Presentation for MSU Staff Council." *Facebook*, 17 Dec. 2019, www.facebook.com/pg/MSUStaffCouncil/posts/.

—. "Soft Skills for STEM." *YouTube*, 27 May 2018, www.youtube.com/watch?v=GkYmMR_IxTY.

Works Consulted

"Artful Listening. Student Research Explores an Unsung Power Skill."
Bentley University, 3 Aug. 2017, www.bentley.edu.

Bauer-Wolf, Jeremy. "Survey: Employers Want 'Soft Skills' from
Graduates." *Inside Higher Ed*, 17 Jan. 2019,
www.insidehighered.com/quicktakes/2019/01/17/
survey-employers-want-soft-skills-graduates.

Bavelas, Janet, Linda Coates, and Trudy Johnson. "Listeners as
Co-Narrators." *Journal of Personality and Social Psychology*,
vol. 79, no. 6, 2000, pp. 941-52. *ResearchGate*,
doi: 10.1037/0022-3514.79.6.941.

Bennett, Art, and Laraine Bennett. *Tuned In: The Power of Pressing
Pause and Listening*. Our Sunday Publishing, 2017.

Bergland, Christopher. "35 Facial Expressions That Convey
Emotions across Cultures." *Psychology Today*, 14 July 2019,
www.psychologytoday.com/us/blog/the-athletes-way/201901/
35-facial-expressions-convey-emotions-across-cultures.

Berry, Jennifer. "Endorphins: Effects and How to Increase Levels."
Medically reviewed by Alana Biggers on 6 Feb. 2018.
Medical News Today, www.medicalnewstoday.com/
articles/320839.

Blake, Daphne. "10 Communication Skills Every Young Professional
Needs to Know." *Hubworks.com*, hubworks.com/blog/
ten-communication-skills-every-young-professional-needs-
to-know.html.

Brown, Claire. "What's the Best, Most Effective Way to Take Notes?" *The Conversation*, 21 May 2015, theconversation.com/whats-the-best-most-effective-way-to-take-notes-41961.

"Build Better Listening Skills." *National Education Association,* www.nea.org/tools/build-better-listening-skills.html.

Carnegie, Dale. *How to Win Friends & Influence People.* Pocket Books, 1981.

Cheung, Theresa. *21 Rituals to Ignite Your Intuition.* Watkins, 2019.

Covey, Stephen R. *The 7 Habits of Highly Effective People.* Simon & Schuster, 2020.

Craighead, Jon. "Artful Listening Raises Productivity, Customer Satisfaction." *Lehigh Valley Business,* 20 Feb. 2017, www.lvb.com/artful-listening-raises-productivity-customer-satisfaction/.

Doidge, Norman. *The Brain That Changes Itself.* Viking, 2007.

Drucker, Peter. *Managing the Non-Profit Organization: Principles and Practices.* HarperCollins, 2006.

Duwe, Morena. "Darly Davis: the Black Musician Who Converts Ku Klux Klan Members." *The Guardian*, 18 Mar. 2020, www.theguardian.com/music/2020/mar/18/daryl-davis-black-musician-who-converts-ku-klux-klan-members.

Finch, David J., Leah K. Hamilton, Riley Baldwin, and Mark Zehner. "An Exploratory Study of Factors Affecting Undergraduate Employability." *Emerald*, 6 Sept. 2013, www.emerald.com/insight/content/doi/10.1108/ET-07-2012-0077/full/html?fullSc=1.

Fitzgerald, Sunny. "6 Ways People around the World Say Hello—without Touching." *National Geographic*, 23 Mar. 2020, www.nationalgeographic.com/travel/2020/03/ways-people-around-world-say-hello-without-touching-coronavirus/.

Forbes Coaches Council. "15 Soft Skills You Need to Succeed When Entering the Workforce." *Forbes*, 22 Jan. 2019, www.forbes.com/sites/forbescoachescouncil/2019/01/22/15-soft-skills-you-need-to-succeed-when-entering-the-workforce/#6da321.

Glass, Don. "Right Ear, Left Ear." *Indiana Public Media*, 24 Feb. 2005, indianapublicmedia.org/amomentofsilence/right-ear-left-ear.php.

Godin, Seth. *Linchpin: Are You Indispensable?* Penguin, 2010.

Goman, Carol Kinsey. "How to Get on the Boss's Good Side—Literally." *Forbes*, 11 June 2012, www.forbes.com/sites/carolkinseygoman/2012/06/11/how-to-get-on-the-bosss-good-side-literally/#1ae092c05ab0.

Groopman, Jerome. *How Doctors Think*. Scribe Publications, 2007.

Harness, Jill. "Proper Business Etiquette for Greeting People." *bizfluent,* 8 May 2019, bizfluent.com/way-5860572-proper-business-etiquette-greeting-people.html.

"Heartbeat." *Cleveland Clinic*, clevelandclinic.org/health/articles/17064-heart-beat.

"How the Ear Works." *University of Maryland Medical Center*, 2020, www.umms.org/ummc/health-services/hearing-balance/patient-information/how-ear-works.

"How to Develop Listening Skills." *WikiHow,* 12 May 2020, wikihow.com.

Jones, Matthew. "10 Ways to Immediately Improve Your Listening (and Networking) Skills." *Inc.,* 10 Jan. 2018, www.inc.com/matthew-jones/10-simple-steps-to-highly-effective-listening.html.

Jordan, William George. *The Majesty of Calmness.* Digireads.com Publishing, 2009.

Lee, Dick, and Delmar Hatesohl. "Listening: Our Most Used Communication Skill." *Communications,* mospace.umsystem.edu/xmlui/bitstream/handle/10355/71861/CM150-1983.pdf?sequence=1.

Lindahl, Kay. *The Sacred Art of Listening: Forty Reflections for Cultivating a Spiritual Practice.* Skylight Paths Publishing, 2001.

"Listen First Conversations." *Listen First Project,* www.listenfirstproject.org/.

Martin, Carole. "Prep for the Top 10 Interview Questions." *United States Probation Office, Southern District of California,* www.casp.uscourts.gov/sites/casp/files/Top%2010%20Interview%20Questions.pdf.

McKay, Dawn Rosenberg. "Listening Skills: How Becoming a Better Listener Will Benefit Your Career." *The Balance Careers,* 28 May 2019, www.thebalancecareers.com/listening-skills-524853.

Meyer, Cheryl. "Boost Your Career with Better Listening Skills." *FM,* 19 Apr. 2019, www.fm-magazine.com/news/2019/apr/improve-your-listening-skills-201920496.html.

Mlodinow, Leonard. "How We Communicate through Body Language: Nonverbal Communication Bestows Advantages in Both Personal and Business Life." *Psychology Today*, 29 May 2012, www.psychologytoday.com/us/blog/sublimina/201205/how-we-communicate-through-body-language.

Murillo, Sandy. "How Does Technology Help People Who Are Blind or Visually Impaired?" *Sandy's View*, 7 May 2015, sandysview1.wordpress.com/2015/05/07/how-does-technology-help-people-who-are-blind-or-visually-impaired/.

Murley, Sean. "New Series to Prompt 'Uncomfortable' Conversations." *The Exponent*, 21 Jan. 2020, www.purdueexponent.org/campus/article_1843a52d-7dc2-5a0b-9e09-bf2e1b229b86.html.

Murphy, Kate. *You're Not Listening: What You're Missing and Why It Matters*. Celadon Books, 2019.

Nichols, Michael P. *The Lost Art of Listening: How Learning to Listen Can Improve Relationships*. Guilford Press, 2009.

Nichols, Ralph G., and Leonard A. Stevens. "Listening to People." *Harvard Business Review*, September 1957, hbr.org/1957/09/listening-to-people.

Peck, Scott M. *The Road Less Traveled: A New Psychology of Love, Traditional Values, and Spiritual Growth*. Simon & Schuster, 1978.

Phelan, Hayley. "What's All This about Journaling?" *New York Times*, 25 Oct. 2018, www.nytimes.com/2018/10/25/style/journaling-benefits.html.

Prater, Meg. "How to Be a Good Car Salesperson." *HubSpot*, 14 Mar. 2019, blog.hubspot.com/sales/how-to-be-a-good-car-salesperson.

Reep, Diana. *Technical Writing*. Pearson, 2011.

"Relaxation Techniques: Breath Control Helps Quell Errant Stress Response." *Harvard Health Publishing*, 6 July 2020, www.health.harvard.edu/mind-and-mood/relaxation-techniques-breath-control-helps-quell-errant-stress-response.

Rogers, Carl R., and F. J. Roethlisberger. "Barriers and Gateways to Communication." *Harvard Business Review*, Nov.-Dec. 1991, hbr.org/1991/11/barriers-and-gateways-to-communication.

Sample, Stephen B., and Warren Bennis. *The Contrarian's Guide to Leadership*. Jossey-Bass, 2001.

Schwantes, Marcel. "The Forgotten Skill That Will Make You a Better Leader." *Inc.*, 25 Feb. 2016, www.inc.com/marcel-schwantes/the-hidden-power-of-this-forgotten-leadership-skill.html.

"7 Sales Questions to Ask Customers Looking to Buy a Car." *USA TODAY*, 10 June 2019, sitelaunch2.com/usatodayclassifieds/7-sales-questions-to-ask-customers-looking-to-buy-a-car/.

Sheppard, Beth. "Annotated Bibliography: Listening." *ResearchGate*, July 2015, www.researchgate.net/publication/328454616_ANNOTATED_BIBLIOGRAPHY_LISTENING.

Sininger, Yvonne S., and Anajali Bhatara. "Laterality of Basic Auditory Perception." *Laterality*, vol. 17, no. 2, Mar. 2012, pp. 129-49.

Stephens, Greg J., Lauren J. Silbert, and Uri Hasson.
"Speaker-Listener Neural Coupling Underlies
Successful Communication." *PNAS*, 10 Aug. 2010,
vol. 107, no. 32, pp.14425-30,
www.pnas.org/content/pnas/107/32/14425.full.pdf?with-=.

Strauss, Valerie. "The Surprising Thing Google Learned about
Its Employees—and What It Means for Today's Students."
The Washington Post, 20 Dec. 2017,
www.washingtonpost.com/news/answer-
sheet/wp/2017/12/20/the-surprising-thing-
google-learned-about-its-employees-and-
what-it-means-for-todays-students/.

Suttie, Jill. "How Smartphones Are Killing Conversation." *Greater
Good Magazine*, 7 Dec. 2015, greatergood.berkeley.edu/
article/item/how_smartphones_are_killing_conversation.

Thompson, Jeff. "Is Nonverbal Communication a Numbers Game?"
Psychology Today, 30 Sept. 2011, www.psychologytoday.com/
us/blog/beyond-words/201109/is-nonverbal-
communication-numbers-game.

Woodson, Carter Godwin. *The Mis-education of the Negro.*
Wilder, 2016.

Zenger, Jack, and Joseph Folkman. "What Great Listeners
Actually Do." *Harvard Business Review*, 14 July 2016,
hbr.org/2016/07/what-great-listeners-actually-do.